simple

photography by Jean Cazals

ALHAMBRA
EDITIONS

This edition first published in 2009 by
Alhambra Editions
Alhambra House
27-31 Charing Cross Road
London WC2H OLS

Editor Anne McDowall
Production Marina Asenjo
Text and photographs © 1999 Quadrille Publishing Limited
and BBC Worldwide
Design and layout © 2004 Quadrille Publishing Limited

Some of the material in this volume was previously published as **Easy Food**.

Cataloguing in Publication Data: a catalogue record for this book is available
from the British Library.

ISBN 978 184400 809 4
Printed in China

Cookery notes
All spoon measures are level: 1 tsp = 5ml spoon; 1 tbsp = 15ml spoon.
Use fresh herbs and freshly ground black pepper unless otherwise suggested.
Free-range eggs are recommended and large eggs should be used except
where a different size is specified. Recipes with raw or lightly cooked eggs
should be avoided by anyone who is pregnant or in a vulnerable health group.

Contents

simple soups and snacks

Chilled tomato soup with Thai flavours

Serves 6

700g/1½lb ripe tomatoes
2 garlic cloves, crushed
1 tsp grated fresh root ginger
4 lime leaves, shredded
2–4 red chillies, seeded and diced
2 spring onions, trimmed and chopped
2 tbsp chopped fresh coriander
300ml/½ pint iced water
150ml/¼ pint tomato juice
2 tbsp light soy sauce
2 tbsp rice wine vinegar
1 tbsp sesame oil
salt and pepper

To serve

ice cubes
torn coriander leaves
sesame oil

1 Roughly chop the tomatoes and place in a blender with the garlic, ginger, lime leaves, chillies, spring onions and coriander. Purée until fairly smooth.
2 Transfer to a large bowl and whisk in the water, tomato juice, soy sauce, wine vinegar and sesame oil. Season with salt and pepper to taste. Cover and chill in the refrigerator for several hours.
3 Serve with ice cubes, garnished with coriander and a drizzle of sesame oil.

An adaptation of classic Spanish gazpacho, using Thai ingredients. Make it during the summer, when tomatoes are full of flavour.

Pea soup with minted gremolata

Illustrated on previous pages

Serves 4
25g/1oz butter
1 onion, diced
1 potato, peeled and diced
450g/1lb shelled fresh peas (see note)
700ml/1¼ pints vegetable or chicken
  stock
2 fresh mint sprigs
salt and pepper

For the gremolata
2 tbsp shredded fresh mint leaves
grated rind of 1–2 lemons
1 garlic clove, crushed
To serve
extra virgin olive oil

1 Melt the butter in a pan, add the onion and potato and fry gently for
10 minutes until softened and lightly golden. Add the peas, stock, mint
and seasoning. Bring to the boil, lower the heat, cover and simmer gently
for 20 minutes.
2 Meanwhile, mix the gremolata ingredients together in a bowl.
3 Transfer the soup to a blender and purée until very smooth. Return
to the pan and heat through. Adjust the seasoning to taste.
4 Spoon the soup into warm bowls and serve topped with the gremolata
and a drizzle of olive oil.

Note Use frozen peas when fresh ones are out of season.

Gremolata – an Italian mix of mint, lemon zest
and garlic – adds a real zing to this creamy,
fresh-tasting soup.

Fennel broth with anchovy croûtes

Serves 6
2 tbsp olive oil
1 onion, sliced
4 garlic cloves, crushed
grated rind of ½ orange
1 tbsp chopped fresh thyme
2 fennel bulbs, thinly sliced
2 tbsp Pernod
400g can chopped tomatoes
900ml/1½ pints fish stock

For the croûtes
6 thin slices French bread
50g/2oz can anchovy fillets, drained
  and chopped
25g/1oz pine nuts
1 garlic clove, crushed
2 tsp lemon juice
pepper
To finish
4 tbsp crème fraîche
fennel fronds or dill, to garnish

1 Preheat oven to 200C/fan oven 180C/Gas 6. Heat the olive oil in a saucepan, add the onion, garlic, orange rind, thyme and fennel, and fry gently for 10 minutes until the onion is softened and lightly golden. Add the Pernod and allow to bubble until it is evaporated.
2 Add the chopped tomatoes and stock, bring to the boil, cover and simmer gently for 30 minutes.
3 Meanwhile make the croûtes. Put the slices of French bread on a baking sheet and bake for 10 minutes until crisp and golden. Set aside.
4 Put the anchovy fillets, pine nuts, garlic, lemon juice and pepper in a blender or food processor and purée until fairly smooth. Spread the anchovy paste on top of the croûtes.
5 Spoon the fennel soup into warmed bowls and top each serving with an anchovy croûte. Add a spoonful of crème fraîche and garnish with a sprinkling of chopped fennel fronds or dill.

A fragrant fennel and fish broth topped with savoury anchovy croûtes.

Roasted tomato soup with ricotta

Serves 6

8 tbsp olive oil

1 onion, finely chopped

900g/2lb ripe tomatoes, halved

12 garlic cloves, peeled

15g/½oz fresh mint leaves

1 tsp caster sugar

salt and pepper

600ml/1 pint vegetable stock

100g/4oz dried pastina (small soup pasta)

For the garnish

50g/2oz ricotta cheese, crumbled

mint leaves

olive oil, to drizzle

1 Preheat oven to 220C/fan oven 200C/Gas 7. Heat half the oil in a shallow flameproof casserole and fry the onion for 10 minutes. Add the tomatoes, garlic cloves, mint, sugar, salt and pepper. Bring to the boil.

2 Transfer to the oven and roast, uncovered, for 20 minutes. Let cool slightly, then purée the tomato mixture with the remaining oil in a blender or food processor; return to the pan.

3 Stir in the stock and bring to the boil. Add the pasta and simmer gently for 10 minutes until al dente. Adjust the seasoning to taste.

4 Spoon into warmed bowls and top with crumbled ricotta, mint leaves and a generous drizzling of olive oil. Serve with Italian bread.

Roasted tomatoes give this hearty Italian tomato soup a great depth of flavour.

Smoked fish tartlets

Serves 8

450g/1lb ready-made shortcrust
pastry
450g/1lb undyed smoked haddock
fillet, skinned
200ml/7fl oz milk
2 strips of lemon zest

200ml/7fl oz double cream
2 medium eggs, lightly beaten
1 tbsp chopped fresh tarragon
pinch of cayenne pepper
salt and pepper
tarragon leaves, to garnish
salad leaves, to serve

1 Preheat oven to 200C/fan oven 180C/Gas 6. Divide the pastry into 8 pieces. Roll out on a lightly floured surface into thin rounds and use to line eight 10cm/4in individual flan tins. Prick the bases with a fork and chill in the refrigerator for 30 minutes.

2 Line the pastry cases with greaseproof paper and baking beans and bake blind for 15 minutes; remove the paper and beans and bake for a further 10–15 minutes until the pastry is crisp and golden. Set aside to cool.

3 Place the fish in a shallow pan with the milk and lemon strips. Bring to a gentle simmer, cover and poach gently for 7 minutes. Cool slightly, then flake the fish discarding any bones. Leave to cool.

4 Put the fish in a bowl with the cream, eggs, tarragon, cayenne and salt and pepper. Stir gently to mix.

5 Spoon the filling into the flan cases and bake for 25 minutes until risen and set. Leave to cool slightly for a few minutes. Serve warm on a bed of mixed salad leaves, garnished with tarragon sprigs.

Smoked fish works beautifully in these melt-in-the-mouth tartlets.

Smoked chicken and sweet onion wrap

Serves 4
1 tbsp olive oil
1 large red onion, sliced
1 red chilli, seeded and sliced
½ tsp salt
50g/2oz redcurrant jelly
1 tbsp red wine vinegar
4 large flour tortillas

2 handfuls of mizuna or other salad
  leaves
225g/8oz smoked chicken (or cooked
  breast fillet), shredded
1 small ripe avocado, peeled, stoned
  and sliced
4 tbsp crème fraîche

1 Heat the oil in a frying pan, add the onion and chilli and fry over a medium heat for 10 minutes until browned. Add the salt, redcurrant jelly, vinegar and 1 tbsp water; cook gently for a further 15 minutes until thickened. Leave to cool.

2 Lay the tortillas flat and then top each one with a few salad leaves, the shredded chicken, avocado slices, a spoonful of the onion jam and a dollop of crème fraîche.

3 Carefully fold the tortilla around the filling to form a cone shape and wrap up firmly. Serve at once or wrap securely in napkins or waxed paper and keep in a cool place until ready to serve.

The sandwich of the moment, 'the wrap' is simply a tasty filling wrapped up in a Mexican soft flour tortilla.

Roasted chicken and spinach wrap

Serves 4
225g/8oz roasted chicken (off the
  bone)
4 large flour tortillas
50g/2oz young spinach leaves, stems
  removed
2 fresh peaches, halved, stoned and
  sliced
2 tbsp mayonnaise
2 tsp chopped fresh basil
freshly grated Parmesan, to taste

1 Cut the roast chicken into long, thin shreds.
2 Lay the tortillas flat on a clean surface and top each one with a handful
of spinach leaves. Scatter the shredded chicken and peach slices on top.
3 Mix the mayonnaise with the chopped basil and spoon on top of the
chicken. Grate over fresh Parmesan to taste.
4 Carefully fold the tortilla around the filling to form a cone shape and wrap
up firmly. Serve at once or wrap securely in waxed paper and keep in
a cool place until ready to serve.

Flour tortillas wrapped around a filling of
shredded chicken, tender spinach, peach slices
and chopped basil for a portable snack.

Pork and liver pâté with apple relish

Serves 4

100g/4oz chicken livers, diced
3 tbsp marsala
175g/6oz unsalted butter
3 shallots, finely chopped
2 garlic cloves, crushed
1 tbsp chopped fresh sage
¼ tsp cayenne pepper
100ml/3½fl oz pork or chicken stock
25g/1oz fresh breadcrumbs
225g/8oz cooked pork, diced

100g/4oz cooked ham, diced
salt and pepper
1 fresh sage sprig
For the apple relish
1 small onion, sliced
½ tsp grated fresh root ginger
1 large cooking apple, peeled, cored and diced
4 tbsp cider vinegar
4 tbsp water
5 tbsp light muscovado sugar

1 Put the chicken livers and marsala in a bowl, and leave to marinate for at least 15 minutes.
2 Melt 50g/2oz of the butter in a frying pan, add the shallots, garlic and sage and fry gently for 5 minutes. Add the chicken livers and marsala. Fry over a high heat for 1 minute, then stir in the cayenne and stock. Simmer for 3–4 minutes until the livers are cooked. Leave to cool completely.
3 Put the cooled mixture in a food processor with the breadcrumbs, pork and ham; work briefly to chop finely. Season to taste.
4 Spoon the mixture into a pâté dish and smooth the surface. Melt remaining butter over a low heat, let cool for 5 minutes, then carefully pour over the pâté. Position the sage sprig on top, pressing gently down into the butter. Chill for several hours.
5 Meanwhile, make the relish. Put all the ingredients in a pan and bring to the boil. Lower heat and simmer for 35–40 minutes until thickened. Cool and season to taste.
6 Serve the pâté with the relish and crisp French sticks.

A simple pâté set under a layer of butter, served with a tangy apple and ginger relish.

Bresaola antipasto

Illustrated on previous pages

Serves 4

50g/2oz good quality, large salted
   capers
1 tbsp plain flour
3 tbsp olive oil
3 tbsp fresh parsley leaves
squeeze of lemon juice
16 slices good quality bresaola
85g/3oz mixed mâche and rocket
   leaves
25g/1oz pecorino cheese shavings

For the dressing

½ small shallot, finely chopped
1 tsp white wine vinegar
½ tsp Dijon mustard
½ tsp sugar
4 tbsp extra virgin olive oil
salt and pepper

1 Soak the capers in cold water for 30 minutes. Drain and pat dry with
kitchen paper, then dust with the flour.
2 Heat the oil in a small frying pan and fry the capers for 2–3 minutes
until crisp and golden. Add the parsley leaves and fry for 30 seconds.
Drain on kitchen paper, then toss the mixture with the lemon juice.
3 Whisk the dressing ingredients together in a bowl.
4 Arrange the bresaola on serving plates. Top with the salad leaves, caper
mixture and pecorino shavings. Drizzle with the dressing and serve.

Cured beef, crisp capers and sweet/sharp
pecorino cheese combine beautifully in this
Italian starter.

Smoked duck antipasto

Serves 4

1 large smoked duck breast
75g/3oz mizuna or rocket leaves
50g/2oz bean sprouts
handful of coriander leaves
2 tsp toasted sesame seeds

For the dressing

2 tbsp sunflower oil
½ tsp sesame oil
1 tbsp lime juice
1¼ tsp caster sugar
1 red chilli, seeded and chopped
salt

1 Thinly slice the duck breast and arrange on individual serving plates.
2 Top each serving with a handful of mizuna or rocket leaves, bean sprouts, a few coriander leaves and a sprinkling of toasted sesame seeds.
3 For the dressing, whisk together the sunflower oil, sesame oil, lime juice, caster sugar, red chilli and a pinch of salt.
4 Drizzle the dressing over the salads to serve.

Note If you are unable to buy whole smoked duck breast, look for a pack of sliced smoked duck breast in the supermarket chilled cabinet.

Fresh coriander, beansprouts, chilli and sesame flavours give this unusual antipasto an oriental twist.

Chicken liver and blueberry salad

Serves 4
4 tbsp extra virgin olive oil
50g/2oz whole unblanched almonds
sea salt and pepper
350g/12oz chicken livers, halved
    if large
175g/6oz blueberries
1 tbsp raspberry vinegar
100g/4oz mixed salad leaves
50g/2oz French beans, blanched
few fresh herb leaves (eg. basil,
    mint, parsley)

1 Heat 2 tbsp oil in a frying pan and fry the almonds gently until evenly browned. Remove with a slotted spoon, dust with sea salt and set aside.
2 Increase the heat. Add the chicken livers to the pan and fry for 1 minute. Turn and fry for a further 1 minute until browned on the outside, but still slightly pink in the middle. Remove and let rest for a few minutes.
3 Return the pan to the heat, add the blueberries and warm through for 30 seconds. Remove from the heat and add the remaining oil and the raspberry vinegar.
4 Arrange the salad leaves, beans, herbs and almonds on serving plates. Add the chicken livers, then spoon over the blueberries and pan juices. Serve at once, with warm bread.

Blueberries and a warm, fruity dressing perfectly offset rich chicken livers.

simple
pasta

Pasta with chilli pesto

Serves 4

1 large red pepper
50g/2oz fresh basil leaves
1 garlic clove, crushed
2 ripe tomatoes, skinned
2 tbsp pine nuts
3 tbsp sun-dried tomato paste

3 tbsp tomato purée
1 tsp mild chilli powder
few drops of Tabasco sauce
50g/2oz Parmesan cheese, freshly
  grated
150ml/¼ pint light olive oil
450g/1lb dried caserecce or spaghetti

1 Grill the red pepper, turning occasionally, until charred. Cool slightly, then skin, halve and de-seed. Place in a food processor with the other ingredients, except the oil and pasta. Work until almost smooth. Turn into a bowl and stir in the oil.

2 Bring a large pan of salted water to the boil. Then add the pasta and cook until al dente.

3 Drain the pasta, keeping back 2 tbsp water in the pan. Immediately toss with chilli pesto to taste, allowing approximately 2 tbsp per serving.

Note Store any leftover pesto in a jar, covered with a layer of olive oil, in the fridge for up to 2 weeks. It is excellent with grilled chicken.

This robust pasta dish is spiked with a fiery homemade chilli pesto – to delicious effect.

Fusilli with fennel and red onion

Illustrated on previous pages

Serves 4

1 fennel bulb, trimmed, cored and
  finely diced
500g/1lb 2oz ripe plum tomatoes,
  seeded and finely diced
1 red onion, finely diced
2 tbsp chopped fresh basil
2 tbsp chopped fresh dill
3 tbsp extra virgin olive oil

juice of 1 lemon
salt and pepper
450g/1lb dried fusilli (preferably
  corn pasta)
basil leaves and red onion slices,
  to garnish
freshly grated Parmesan cheese,
  to serve

1 In a bowl, mix together the fennel, tomatoes, red onion, herbs, olive oil and lemon juice. Season with salt and pepper to taste and set aside.
2 Cook the pasta in a large pan of boiling salted water until al dente.
3 Drain the pasta, and return to the pan. Add the fennel sauce and toss to mix. Check the seasoning. Cover with a lid and then leave to stand for 2–3 minutes to allow the flavours to infuse.
4 Serve garnished with basil and red onion slices. Accompany with some grated Parmesan.

Fresh fennel, dill, red onion, tomatoes and herbs give this uncooked sauce a wonderfully refreshing taste.

Spaghetti with aubergines

Serves 4–6
900g/2lb aubergines, cut into
  1cm/½in dice
salt and pepper
5 tbsp olive oil
2–3 tbsp crushed sun-dried tomatoes
  in oil

1 tbsp finely shredded fresh basil
  leaves
500g/1lb 2oz dried spaghetti
75g/2½oz pine nuts, toasted
freshly grated pecorino or Parmesan
  cheese, to serve

1 Put the aubergines in a colander and sprinkle generously with salt.
Leave to drain for 30 minutes. Rinse well and pat dry on a tea towel.
2 Heat the oil in a pan and fry the aubergines for about 15 minutes, until
tender and brown. Add the sun-dried tomatoes, basil and pepper.
3 Meanwhile, cook the spaghetti in a large pan of boiling salted water until
al dente. Drain and toss with the aubergine mixture and pine nuts. Serve
at once, with grated pecorino or Parmesan.

Note It is worth salting the aubergines for this dish, to draw out their
bitter juices.

Spaghetti tossed with a rustic sauce of fried
aubergine, crushed sun-dried tomato and
toasted pine nuts. Serve with a rocket salad.

Pasta with courgettes and mushrooms

Serves 4
450g/1lb dried curly pasta shapes, such as spiralli or caserecce, or shells
salt and pepper
50g/2oz butter

1 garlic clove, chopped
4–6 large flat mushrooms, sliced
1 tbsp chopped fresh thyme
4 small courgettes, coarsely grated
pecorino or Parmesan cheese shavings, to serve

1 Bring a large pan of salted water to the boil. Add the pasta and cook until al dente.

2 Meanwhile, melt the butter in a frying pan. Add the garlic and cook gently for 2–3 minutes until golden.

3 Add the sliced mushrooms and fry for about 2 minutes until softened and beginning to brown.

4 Stir in the thyme and grated courgettes. Increase the heat and cook, stirring constantly, for about 5 minutes or until the courgettes are tender. Season with salt and pepper to taste.

5 Drain the pasta, keeping 2 tbsp water in the pan. Immediately toss the pasta with the sauce and serve topped with pecorino or Parmesan shavings.

Note For speed, use a food processor fitted with a coarse grating disc to prepare the courgettes, or dice them if you prefer.

Variation Use 175g (6oz) button or chestnut mushrooms instead of flat mushrooms.

Mushrooms and courgettes are perfect partners. Sautéed with garlic and thyme, they make a wonderful aromatic sauce.

Penne with roasted beetroot and feta

Serves 4
450g/1lb baby beetroot, trimmed
  (see note)
1 garlic clove, crushed
2 tbsp walnut oil, plus extra to
  drizzle
salt and pepper

300g/10oz dried penne or other
  pasta shapes
50g/2oz rocket leaves
100g/4oz feta cheese, crumbled
2 tbsp toasted pine nuts
pecorino or Parmesan cheese,
  to serve

1 Preheat oven to 220C/fan oven 200C/Gas 7. Put the beetroot in a small roasting tin with the garlic, oil, salt and pepper. Add 2 tbsp water and roast in the oven for 50–60 minutes until tender. Keep warm.
2 Cook the pasta in a large pan of boiling salted water until al dente.
3 Drain the pasta thoroughly and immediately toss with the rocket leaves, roasted beetroot, pepper and a little extra walnut oil.
4 Spoon the pasta mixture into warmed bowls and scatter over the crumbled feta and toasted pine nuts. Drizzle with walnut oil to serve.

Note To ensure the baby beets are similar in size, halve any larger ones.

Sweet roasted beetroot and salty feta combine well in this pretty pasta dish. The rocket just wilts as it is stirred into the hot pasta.

Tomato spaghetti with coriander and avocado

Illustrated on previous pages

Serves 4

500g/1lb 2oz cherry tomatoes,
   quartered
2 tbsp torn fresh coriander leaves
grated rind and juice of ½ lemon
1 garlic clove, crushed
3 tbsp extra virgin olive oil
3 small avocados (preferably hass),
   peeled, stoned and cut into
   1cm/½in dice
salt and pepper
450g/1lb dried tomato spaghetti

1 Combine the tomatoes, coriander, lemon rind and juice, garlic and olive oil in a large bowl. Add the diced avocados and toss gently to mix. Season with salt and pepper to taste and set aside.

2 Cook the pasta in a large pan of boiling salted water until al dente.

3 Drain the pasta and toss gently with the sauce to serve.

Note Don't prepare this sauce too far in advance, or the avocado may discolour and spoil the appearance of the dish.

The heat of the cooked spaghetti brings out the full flavours of creamy, ripe avocados and cherry tomatoes.

Buckwheat noodles with Savoy cabbage

Serves 4

2 tbsp olive oil

125g/4½oz pancetta or lightly
   smoked bacon, diced

2 red onions, sliced

225g/8oz Savoy cabbage, shredded

3 garlic cloves, chopped

225g/8oz buckwheat (soba) noodles,
   or egg tagliatelle

salt and pepper

250g tub mascarpone cheese

140g/5oz dolcelatte cheese, diced

1 Heat the oil in a large deep frying pan, add the pancetta or bacon and
onions and fry for 5 minutes, stirring occasionally.

2 Stir in the cabbage and garlic, cover and cook for 8–10 minutes until the
cabbage is tender.

3 Meanwhile, cook the noodles in a large pan of boiling salted water until
al dente.

4 Drain the noodles thoroughly and toss with the cabbage; season. Add the
cheeses and heat gently until they melt to a creamy sauce. Serve immediately.

Japanese noodles tossed with pancetta and
cabbage in a creamy cheese sauce.

Spaghetti, peas and oven-dried tomatoes

Serves 4–6
500g/1lb 2oz dried spaghetti
salt and pepper
450g/1lb frozen or fresh peas or
   petits pois
1 batch oven-dried tomatoes
   (see below)
2 tbsp finely shredded fresh mint

1 Cook the spaghetti in a large pan of boiling salted water until al dente.
2 Meanwhile, cook the peas in a separate pan of boiling water until tender.
3 Drain the pasta and peas, return to the warm pasta pan and add the oven-dried tomatoes with 2–3 tbsp of the oil, and the mint. Toss lightly, season and serve.

Oven-dried tomatoes Preheat oven to 130C/fan oven 110C/Gas 1. Lay 400g/14oz halved cherry tomatoes on a non-stick baking tray cut-side up. Sprinkle with salt, pepper and sugar. Bake for 1½ hours or until dry but not brown. Cool slightly, then put into a bowl and add extra virgin olive oil to cover. When cold, store in jars covered with a layer of olive oil. Use as required.

Oven-dried cherry tomatoes bring a sweet intensity to this dish.

Tagliatelle with wild mushroom sauce

Serves 4

20g/³⁄₄oz dried porcini mushrooms
150ml/¼ pint dry white wine
3 garlic cloves, peeled
300ml/½ pint double cream
50g/2oz walnuts
2 tbsp olive oil

400g/14oz mixed oyster, chestnut
and wild or field mushrooms
salt and pepper
375g/13oz dried egg tagliatelle
cep powder, to sprinkle (optional,
see note)
chervil sprigs, to garnish

1 Soak the dried porcini in the wine for 30 minutes to soften. Strain the soaking liquid into a small heavy-based pan, squeezing out all excess liquid from the porcini.

2 Add the garlic to the pan and simmer until softened and the liquid is reduced by half; take out the garlic and set aside. Stir the cream into the liquid; remove from the heat.

3 Chop the garlic, nuts and porcini together, to a coarse paste. Heat the oil in a wok or deep frying pan and stir-fry the mushrooms (halved if large) over a high heat, adding firmer ones first. Season well. Lower the heat and stir in the walnut paste, then the sauce; heat through.

4 Add the tagliatelle to a large pan of boiling salted water and cook until al dente. Drain well and toss the pasta with the mushroom sauce. Serve dusted with cep powder if wished, and scattered with chervil.

Note Cep powder adds a special finishing touch. It is available in a shaker from larger supermarkets or, to make your own, grind dried ceps to a powder in a coffee grinder.

Locate a good selection of mushrooms, including wild ones if possible. Use mushroom-flavoured tagliatelle if preferred.

Pasta with bacon and wilted spinach

Serves 4
450g/1lb dried spaghetti, tagliatelle
  or linguine
salt and pepper
4 tbsp olive oil
8 slices pancetta or unsmoked
  streaky bacon, chopped

2 garlic cloves, finely chopped
900g/2lb spinach leaves, stalks
  removed
150ml/¼ pint double cream
freshly grated nutmeg
3 tbsp pine nuts, toasted

1 Bring a large pan of salted water to the boil. Add the pasta and cook until al dente.

2 Meanwhile heat the oil in a large pan, add the pancetta or bacon and fry until just turning golden. Add the garlic and cook for 1 minute.

3 Stir in the spinach and cook over a high heat for a few minutes or until the leaves are just wilted. Pour in the cream, turning the spinach to ensure it is well coated. Season with salt, pepper and nutmeg. Heat until boiling.

4 Drain the pasta, keeping back 2 tbsp water in the pan. Immediately toss the pasta with the hot sauce. Serve sprinkled with the pine nuts.

Bacon, garlic and spinach are mellowed in a cream sauce. Don't overcook the fresh spinach – it should be vivid green and full of flavour.

Pasta with garlic and anchovy sauce

Serves 4
3 tbsp olive oil
3 garlic cloves, chopped
1 small can anchovies in oil, drained
    and chopped
400g can chopped tomatoes
pepper
450g/1lb dried bucatini, macaroni or
    pasta shapes
10 large fresh basil leaves, shredded
100g/4oz fresh rocket leaves

1 Heat the olive oil in a saucepan. Add the garlic and fry until just colouring. Stir in the anchovies and cook gently until they begin to dissolve.
2 Stir in the chopped tomatoes and bring to the boil. Season to taste with pepper (salt won't be needed as the anchovies are quite salty). Cover and simmer gently for 10 minutes.
3 Meanwhile, bring a large pan of salted water to the boil. Add the pasta and cook until al dente. Drain the pasta, keeping back 2 tbsp water in the pan.
4 Stir the shredded basil into the tomato and anchovy sauce. Immediately add to the pasta and toss well. Serve each portion topped with a tangle of rocket leaves.

Pasta in a classic tomato sauce infused with the savoury saltiness of melted anchovies, topped with contrasting peppery rocket.

Macaroni bakes with balsamic vinegar

Serves 4

100g/4oz dried elbow macaroni

salt and pepper

300ml/½ pint double cream

50g/2oz gruyère cheese, grated

25g/1oz Parmesan cheese, freshly
  grated

3 eggs, beaten

For the dressing

1 shallot, finely diced

2 ripe tomatoes, peeled, seeded and
  diced

6 tbsp extra virgin olive oil

few fresh thyme leaves

1 tbsp balsamic vinegar

1 Preheat oven to 180C/fan oven 160C/Gas 4. Oil and base line 4 timbales
or ovenproof cups.

2 Cook the pasta in boiling salted water until al dente. Drain thoroughly
and divide between the timbales or cups.

3 Slowly bring the cream to the boil in a pan. Remove from the heat, season
and stir in the cheeses until melted. Stir into the beaten eggs. Pour the
savoury custard over the macaroni.

4 Stand the moulds in a roasting tin, half filled with boiling water. Bake
for 25 minutes.

5 Remove the moulds from the bain-marie; let rest for 5 minutes. Warm
the dressing ingredients together in a small pan for 5 minutes or until the
shallots are softened; season with salt and pepper to taste.

6 Turn out the pasta moulds onto warmed plates and surround with the
tomato dressing. Garnish with thyme to serve.

Macaroni baked in a savoury cheese custard
in timbales, then turned out and served with
a piquant tomato sauce.

simple
fish

Peppered salmon with juniper and vermouth

Serves 4
1 tsp dried green peppercorns
16 juniper berries
1 tsp salt
4 salmon steaks or fillets, skinned
25g/1oz unsalted butter
8 tbsp dry vermouth (preferably
  Noilly Prat)
2–3 tbsp double cream or crème
  fraîche

1 Crush together the peppercorns, juniper berries and salt, using a pestle and mortar (or end of a rolling pin and strong bowl). Sprinkle over the salmon and press well to adhere.
2 Melt the butter in a frying pan over a medium heat and fry the seasoned fish for about 10–12 minutes for steaks, a little less for salmon fillets, turning once.
3 Lift the salmon onto a warm serving dish; keep warm while you finish the sauce.
4 Deglaze the pan with the vermouth and let bubble for 2–3 minutes until syrupy. Stir in the cream or crème fraîche and let bubble for 2 minutes. Spoon the sauce over the salmon to serve.

Note If buying salmon by the piece to cut into portions, choose the middle or tail end as this is less oily than the head end.

An easy dish with intriguing flavours – delicious with herby mashed potatoes.

Basque baked fish in parchment

Illustrated on previous pages

Serves 4

4 cod or haddock fillets, each
175–200g/6–7oz, skinned
½ green pepper, cored, seeded and
diced
½ red pepper, cored, seeded and diced
1 onion, finely chopped
1 tbsp fresh oregano leaves, chopped

2 garlic cloves, finely chopped
2 plum tomatoes, skinned, seeded
and chopped
juice of 1 lemon
1 tbsp olive oil
4 tbsp dry white wine
salt and pepper
12 black olives (optional)

1 Preheat oven to 190C/fan oven 170C/Gas 5. Cut 4 sheets of non-stick baking parchment, measuring approximately 30x38cm/12x15in. Place each fish fillet on a piece of paper, positioning it slightly off centre.

2 In a bowl, mix together the peppers, onion, oregano, garlic, tomatoes, lemon juice, olive oil and wine. Season with salt and pepper.

3 Spoon the mixture on top of the fish and scatter over the olives, if using. Fold the parchment over the fish to form a triangle. Fold the edges together tightly to form a sealed parcel.

4 Lift the parcels onto a baking sheet and bake for 15–20 minutes until the fish is cooked through. Place each parcel on a warmed plate and serve at once, with buttery new potatoes and steamed broccoli.

These fish parcels cook quickly and easily in the oven, trapping in the flavours of sweet peppers, onion, garlic and oregano.

Portuguese fish and potato bake

Serves 4

750g/1lb 10oz thick cod fillets, skinned

5 tbsp olive oil

3 large onions, halved and thinly sliced

3 garlic cloves, finely chopped

600g/1lb 5oz potatoes (King Edward or Desiree)

3 tbsp finely chopped fresh parsley

16 black olives, stoned and roughly chopped

salt and pepper

150ml/¼ pint fish or chicken stock

For the garnish

4 hard-boiled eggs, quartered

chopped flat leaf parsley

1 Preheat oven to 180C/fan oven 160C/Gas 4. Place the fish fillets on a lightly oiled baking sheet, brush with olive oil and bake for 7–10 minutes. Let cool slightly.

2 Meanwhile, heat the remaining oil in a large frying pan, add the onions and sauté for about 20 minutes until golden brown. Add the garlic and sauté for 2 minutes; set aside.

3 In the meantime, boil the potatoes until tender. Drain and leave to cool slightly, then peel and cut into 1cm/½in slices.

4 When the fish is cool enough to handle, separate into large flakes.

5 Lightly oil a shallow ovenproof dish, 24–25cm/9½–10in in diameter. Layer the potatoes, onions, parsley, olives and fish in the dish, seasoning each layer generously and finishing with a layer of onions. Pour in the stock and bake for 20 minutes.

6 Serve garnished with hard-boiled eggs and chopped parsley. Accompany with green beans or roasted tomatoes.

Flavoured with caramelised onions, black olives and garlic, this tasty bake is best enjoyed with a glass of Rioja.

Warm smoked haddock and butter bean salad

Serves 4

4 small cooked beetroot, diced
2 tsp cider vinegar
500g/1lb 2oz undyed smoked
    haddock fillet, skinned
1 bunch watercress, trimmed
400g can butter beans, drained
3 spring onions, finely sliced
pepper

1 Toss the diced beetroot in the cider vinegar; set aside.
2 Poach the haddock in just sufficient water to cover for 4–5 minutes until opaque; drain.
3 Meanwhile gently mix the watercress sprigs, butter beans, onions and beetroot together in a shallow serving bowl.
4 When the fish is cool enough to handle, divide into flakes and scatter over the salad. Season with plenty of pepper.

Note The beetroot lightly tinges the beans a pretty pale pink. Combine the salad shortly before serving to avoid over-colouring.

Smoked haddock marries with sweet beetroot and creamy butter beans to make a satisfying meal that is low in fat.

Smoked mackerel and spinach frittata

Illustrated on previous pages

Serves 3–4

450g/1lb ready-prepared young
   fresh spinach
2 tbsp olive oil
225g/8oz smoked mackerel fillets
175g/6oz small new potatoes

salt and pepper
100g/4oz butter
6 large eggs
50g/2oz Parmesan cheese, freshly
   grated

1 Remove any tough stems from the spinach. Heat the oil in a frying pan, add the spinach and toss until just wilted; transfer to a plate. Remove the skin from the mackerel fillets and roughly flake the flesh.

2 Cook the potatoes in boiling salted water for 15–20 minutes until just tender. Drain and allow to cool slightly, then slice thickly.

3 Heat half the butter in a non-stick frying pan and sauté the potatoes for 5 minutes or until beginning to colour.

4 In a bowl, beat the eggs with half of the Parmesan, a good pinch of salt and plenty of pepper. Stir in the spinach and potatoes.

5 Melt the remaining butter in a 25cm/10in heavy non-stick frying pan. When foaming, pour in the egg mixture. Turn down the heat as low as possible. Cook for about 15 minutes until set, with the top still a little runny. Scatter over the flaked mackerel and sprinkle with the remaining Parmesan.

6 Place briefly under a hot grill to lightly brown the cheese and just set the top; do not overbrown or the frittata will dry out. Slide onto a warm plate and cut into wedges. Serve with a crisp salad.

This Italian omelette is cooked slowly and the filling is stirred into the eggs or scattered on top. A frittata is served just set, never folded.

Pan-fried monkfish with Dijon mustard

Serves 4

40g/1½oz unsalted butter
2 monkfish fillets, each about
 300g/10oz, skinned and thickly
 sliced
1 garlic clove, crushed
100ml/3½fl oz extra dry white
 vermouth
1 tbsp Dijon mustard
150ml/¼ pint double cream
1 tbsp snipped fresh chives (optional)

1 Melt the butter in a large frying pan and briefly fry the monkfish for
1–2 minutes until almost cooked. Lift from the pan.
2 Add the garlic to the pan and fry gently until softened. Add the vermouth
and mustard and bubble vigorously to boil off the alcohol.
3 Stir in the cream, and chives if using, then return the fish to the pan
to warm through and finish cooking. Serve with tagliatelle and sugar snap
peas or mangetout.

Flash-fried monkfish slices in a creamy
mustard sauce with a dash of vermouth.

Herring with mustard-lemon butter

Serves 4
100g/4oz pinhead oatmeal
grated rind and juice of 1 lemon
4 large herring fillets
100ml/3½fl oz milk
50g/2oz butter
1 lemon, thinly sliced
1 tbsp wholegrain mustard
2 tbsp chopped fresh parsley
salt and pepper

1 Mix the oatmeal with the lemon rind. Dip the herring into the milk, then into the oatmeal to coat on both sides.
2 Melt the butter in a large frying pan and fry the herring fillets with the lemon slices for about 2 minutes on each side; transfer to warm plates and keep warm.
3 Add the lemon juice, mustard and parsley to the pan and heat until bubbling; season. Pour over the herring and serve.

Fillets of herring are dipped in oatmeal mixed with grated lemon rind, then pan-fried in butter flavoured with lemon and parsley.

Trout with dill cucumbers and capers

Serves 2
2 whole trout, cleaned
2 tbsp seasoned flour
25g/1oz unsalted butter
juice of ½ small lemon
½ dill cucumber, finely chopped
1–2 tsp capers
1–2 tbsp flat leaf parsley, roughly
   chopped
salt and pepper

1 Coat the trout in seasoned flour. Melt the butter in a large frying pan, then fry the trout for 5 minutes each side or until cooked and the skin is crisp. Lift on to warm plates.
2 Pour the lemon juice into the pan juices. Warm through with the cucumber, capers and parsley. Season to taste, then pour over the trout. Serve with a salad and potatoes.

Pan-fried trout with a piquant sauce of lemon butter, capers, dill cucumber and parsley.

Spicy grilled sardines

Serves 4
4 garlic cloves, crushed
½ tsp hot paprika
1 tsp ground cumin
1 tbsp lemon juice
1 tbsp olive oil
salt and pepper
12–16 fresh sardines, depending
   on size, cleaned

For the salad
5 oranges
1 red onion, very thinly sliced
25g/1oz flat leaf parsley leaves,
   roughly torn
16 large black olives (optional)
extra virgin olive oil, for drizzling

1 Mix the garlic with the spices, lemon juice, olive oil and seasoning.
Rub this mixture all over the sardines to coat thoroughly. Set aside.
2 For the salad, peel and segment the oranges, discarding all white pith,
membrane and pips. Place the orange segments in a bowl with the red onion,
chopped parsley and black olives if using. Season with salt and pepper
to taste and drizzle with a little olive oil.
3 Preheat the grill. Place the sardines on the rack over the grill pan and
grill for approximately 2 minutes each side until cooked through. Serve
with the orange salad and warm crusty bread.

Note Before grilling the sardines, add a little water to the grill pan.
This will prevent any juices from the fish burning on the pan base, which
causes smoking.

Fresh sardines are grilled with a spicy garlic
coating and served with a refreshing
Moroccan orange salad.

Mussels steamed in a paper bag

Illustrated on previous pages

Serves 4

1.5kg/3lb 5oz fresh mussels in shells
2 tbsp olive oil
1 garlic clove, chopped
2 celery sticks, cut into fine julienne
    strips

1 red pepper, cored, seeded and
    finely sliced
1 red chilli, seeded and finely diced
1 tsp Szechuan peppercorns, crushed
4 tbsp teriyaki marinade

1 To clean the mussels if necessary, scrub in several changes of water, discarding any that do not close when sharply tapped. Pull off any 'beards' which are still attached.

2 Preheat oven to 230C/fan oven 210C/Gas 8. Heat the oil in a frying pan and add the garlic, celery, red pepper and chilli. Stir-fry over a brisk heat for 1 minute. Add the crushed peppercorns and take off the heat.

3 Cut four 30cm/12in squares of baking parchment. Divide the mussels between the paper squares, piling them in the centre. Top with the stir-fried vegetables and pour 15ml/1 tbsp teriyaki marinade over each portion. Bring the sides of the paper up over the mussels to enclose them like a bag; tie with cotton string. Place on a baking tray.

4 Place in the oven for 10 minutes or until the mussels open (squeeze bags to check). Serve immediately, in the paper bags!

Note Make sure guests discard any mussels which have not opened.

Mussels are quick and easy – especially if you buy ready cleaned ones and cook them in this unusual way.

Salt-baked hake

Serves 2
1 hake, about 600g/1lb 5oz, cleaned
1tbsp Maldon salt flakes
few fresh rosemary branches
lemon wedges, to serve

1 Preheat oven to 220C/fan oven 200C/Gas 7. Snip the fins off the fish, using kitchen scissors. Wash the fish under running cold water. Shake off excess moisture then, holding on to the tail, toss the fish in the salt so that it all adheres.
2 Lay the rosemary over the base of an ovenproof dish and place the fish on top. Immediately bake for about 20 minutes until cooked through.
3 To serve, carefully break away and discard the salted fish skin. Serve the fish accompanied by lemon wedges, warm bread and a tomato, olive and red onion salad.

Hake is an inexpensive white fish with a good flavour. Here it is baked in a salt crust to seal in the flavour and juices. The flesh stays moist and, surprisingly, it isn't too salty.

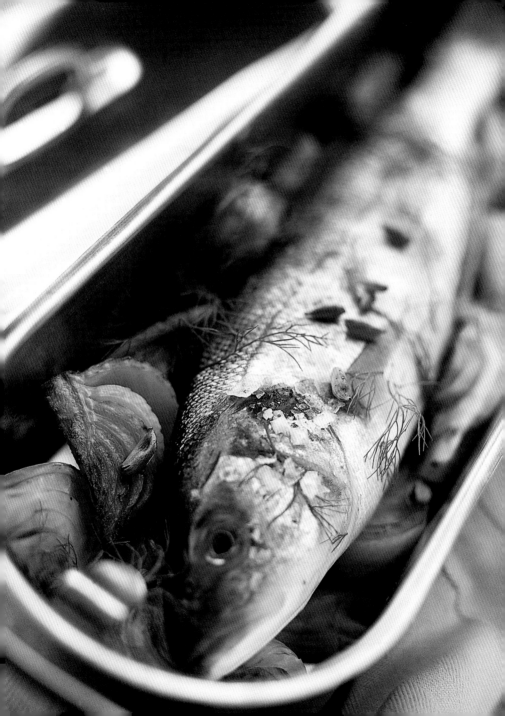

Steamed sea bass
with fennel

Serves 2

1 tbsp olive oil

3 small fennel bulbs, trimmed and
  each cut into 8 wedges, feathery
  fronds reserved

½ tsp cardamom seeds (from 3–4 pods)

500ml/18fl oz vegetable stock

1 sea bass, about 750g/1lb 10oz,
  cleaned

salt and pepper

1 Heat the oil in a wide, heavy based deep pot or flameproof casserole,
add the fennel with the cardamom seeds and fry until lightly browned
and slightly softened.

2 Add the stock and bring to the boil. Lower the heat, cover and simmer
for 10 minutes.

3 Season the fish and place on its side on top of the fennel. Cover tightly
and cook over a medium heat for 15–20 minutes. To make sure the fish is
cooked, insert a knife in the thickest part of the back and check that the
flesh is opaque.

4 Carefully lift the fish on to a serving dish and surround with the fennel
wedges. Spoon the pan juices over the fish and garnish with the reserved
fennel fronds. Serve with warm crusty bread or plain boiled potatoes to mop
up the juices.

Note Most white fish have low fat flesh because their oil is stored in the liver.
Oily fish, such as sardines, salmon, tuna and trout, have oil distributed
throughout their flesh and are therefore relatively high in fat but full of
beneficial fish oils and vitamins.

The delicate flavours in this fragrant one-pot
meal are retained during cooking.

simple
chicken

Goujons with avocado mayonnaise

Serves 4

4 slices softgrain bread

2 tsp poppy seeds

¼ tsp cayenne pepper

2 tbsp snipped fresh chives

4 skinless chicken breast fillets,
   thickly sliced

2 eggs, beaten

4 tbsp sunflower oil, for frying

For the mayonnaise

1 large avocado, halved and stoned

3 tbsp mayonnaise

2 tbsp French dressing

salt and pepper

1 First blend the mayonnaise ingredients together in a food processor until creamy; turn into a bowl. Clean the processor.

2 Break the bread in to the food processor. Add the spices, chives and 1 tsp salt. Process to crumbs; tip on to a plate. Dip the chicken strips in the egg, then into the spicy crumbs to coat.

3 Heat the oil in a large non-stick frying pan and fry the goujons for 2–3 minutes each side until crisp and golden. Serve hot, with the avocado mayonnaise and a salad.

Poppy seeds, chives and cayenne add a savoury note to these crunchy chicken strips. An avocado dip is the perfect foil.

Lemon chicken with garlic and potatoes

Illustrated on previous pages

Serves 4

8–12 chicken pieces (thighs and
   drumsticks)
salt and pepper
finely grated rind of 1 lemon
2 tbsp chopped fresh thyme
900g/2lb small new potatoes
1 lemon, very thinly sliced
12 large garlic cloves (unpeeled)
150ml/¼ pint olive oil

1 Preheat oven to 180C/fan oven 160C/Gas 4. Put the chicken in a large
bowl, season well and add the lemon rind and thyme. Toss well to coat and
spread in a large baking dish.
2 Crack each potato by tapping sharply with a rolling pin. Add to the
chicken. Tuck the lemon slices around. Scatter the garlic cloves over
the chicken. Drizzle the olive oil evenly over the top.
3 Bake for about 45 minutes, stirring occasionally, until golden brown
and cooked through. Serve with courgettes or broccoli.

Try this as an alternative to the traditional
Sunday roast – it's all done in one dish!

Chicken with pancetta and asparagus

Serves 6

150g/51/2oz asparagus tips
6 free-range chicken breast fillets,
   skinned
salt and pepper
18 slices pancetta
2 tbsp olive oil
chervil or parsley sprigs, to garnish

1 Cook the asparagus in boiling water for 2 minutes, then drain and refresh in cold water; drain again and pat dry on kitchen paper.

2 Slice horizontally into each chicken breast without cutting all the way through, then open out. Place, two at a time, between sheets of greaseproof paper and beat with a rolling pin to flatten out slightly.

3 Preheat oven to 190C/fan oven 170C/Gas 5. Season each chicken breast lightly and cover with 1½ slices of pancetta. Place 4 asparagus tips lengthways on top and roll up. Brush the chicken parcels with a little oil and wrap each one in a further 1½ slices of pancetta.

4 Wrap each parcel tightly in foil to seal and hold in the juices. Place on a baking sheet and bake in the oven for 20 minutes.

5 Leave to rest in a warm place for 5–15 minutes, then remove the foil. Slice the chicken parcels into rounds and serve on a bed of rice, with any juices poured over. Garnish with chervil or parsley.

Note Packets of thinly sliced pancetta are available from larger supermarkets. Alternatively you can buy pancetta freshly sliced from Italian delicatessens.

These are very easy to prepare, hours in advance. Serve sliced to reveal the pretty asparagus and pancetta.

Chicken pies with butternut mash

Serves 4

500g/1lb 2oz butternut squash,
  peeled, seeded and diced
1 kg/2lb 4oz potatoes, peeled and
  diced
300ml/½ pint milk
1 tsp chopped fresh sage
25g/1oz butter
salt and pepper

4 skinless chicken breast fillets, cut
  into 2.5cm/1in cubes
1 small Bramley apple, peeled, cored
  and chopped
2 leeks, sliced
150ml/¼ pint dry cider
1 chicken stock cube
50g/2oz mature Cheddar cheese,
  grated

1 Put the butternut squash, potatoes, milk, chopped sage and butter in a pan and season with salt and pepper. Bring to the boil, lower the heat, cover the pan tightly and simmer for 20–25 minutes, stirring once, until the potatoes are tender. Mash until the mixture is smooth.

2 Meanwhile, put the chicken in a pan with the apple, leeks, cider and stock. Season, cover and simmer gently for 25 minutes until the leeks and chicken are tender and the apples are pulpy.

3 Spoon the chicken mixture over the base of four 350ml/12fl oz pie dishes and top with the mash. Sprinkle with the cheese. (If preparing ahead, cover and keep in the fridge until ready to cook.)

4 To serve, preheat oven to 190C/fan oven 170C/Gas 5. Bake the pies for 30 minutes until golden and piping hot. Serve with broccoli or cabbage.

Tasty pies filled with chicken, leeks and tart apple cooked in cider. Butternut squash gives a sweet, nutty flavour to the mash topping.

Skewered rosemary chicken

Serves 4

4 skinless chicken breast fillets, cut
   into 2.5cm/1in cubes
1 clove garlic, crushed
2 tsp chopped fresh thyme
juice of ½ lemon
salt and pepper
8 fresh rosemary stems, at least
   23cm/9in long (preferably woody)

1 Put the chicken in a non-metallic bowl and add the garlic, thyme, lemon juice and seasoning. Toss well and leave to marinate for 30–40 minutes (no longer), turning occasionally.

2 Strip the rosemary stems of their leaves, except for the 7.5cm/3in at the narrow end. Cut the woody ends obliquely to shape points that will pierce the chicken.

3 Preheat the grill. Lift the chicken from the marinade, reserving the juice.

4 Thread the chicken pieces on to the skewers carefully and lay on the grill tray, with the leafy rosemary tips towards you.

5 Cover the rosemary leaves with a strip of foil to prevent them from scorching. Grill for about 10–15 minutes, turning and basting occasionally with the reserved marinade. Serve with a mixed salad.

Note Try using bay or sage branches instead of rosemary – the woodier the herb stems, the better. Or, for a quicker alternative, thread the chicken pieces onto pre-soaked wooden kebab skewers and sprinkle with a little chopped rosemary before grilling.

Grilling meat on herb skewers gives off a wonderful aroma to stimulate the tastebuds.

Lime and ginger grilled chicken

Serves 4

4 skinless chicken breast fillets
½ tsp finely grated lime rind
juice of ½ large lime
2.5 cm/1in piece fresh root ginger,
    finely shredded
salt and pepper
2 tsp maple syrup or clear honey
snipped chives, to garnish

1 Using a very sharp knife, score the chicken deeply in a criss-cross pattern,
cutting halfway through the thickness. Place in a shallow dish.
2 Mix together the lime rind and juice, ginger and seasoning. Brush this
over the scored surface of the chicken and leave to marinate for about
20 minutes.
3 Preheat the grill to high. Brush the chicken with the maple syrup
or honey and cook for 7–8 minutes on each side, turning and basting
at least twice.
4 Serve garnished with snipped chives and accompanied by steamed French
beans or sugar snap peas.

Lean chicken breast fillets are deeply scored
before marinating to encourage the flavours
to permeate and ensure quick cooking.

Rancher's chicken

Serves 2

2 skinless chicken breast fillets
1 large tomato, finely chopped
2 tbsp hickory barbecue sauce
1 tbsp olive oil
4 rindless smoked streaky bacon
   rashers
50g/2oz mature Cheddar cheese,
   grated

1 Beat the chicken fillets with a rolling pin until flattened to an even
thickness. Stir the tomato into the hickory sauce.
2 Heat the oil in a large cast-iron (or other grillproof) frying pan, add the
chicken and bacon and fry for about 1–2 minutes each side. Preheat the
grill.
3 Space the chicken fillets apart in the pan, then spread with the tomato
mixture. Sprinkle with the cheese and top with the bacon.
4 Grill for about 3 minutes until the bacon is turning golden and the cheese
has melted. Serve with a salad and jacket potatoes.

This takes minutes to make, yet the smoky
sauce adds a special taste.

Warm chicken and asparagus salad

Serves 4
300g/10oz medium asparagus,
  trimmed
4 chicken breast fillets, cut into
  strips
1 tbsp vegetable oil
salt and pepper
4 tbsp fresh mint leaves
100g/4oz baby spinach leaves

For the lemon grass dressing:
1 tbsp sesame oil
1 tbsp vegetable oil
1 tsp paprika
2 lemon grass stalks, thinly sliced
3 tbsp lime juice
1 tbsp honey
2 tbsp light soy sauce

1 Preheat the grill to medium. Blanch the asparagus in boiling water for
3 minutes; drain and pat dry.
2 Brush the chicken strips and asparagus with oil; and season with salt
and pepper. Place on the grill rack and grill for 3–4 minutes on each side,
or until the chicken is cooked through.
3 Meanwhile, make the dressing. Gently heat the oils in a small pan. Add
the paprika and lemon grass and cook for 1–2 minutes.
4 Arrange the mint and spinach leaves on plates and top with the asparagus
and chicken.
5 Add the lime juice, honey and soy sauce to the dressing and slowly bring
to a simmer. Pour the warm dressing over the salad to serve.

Note Char-grill the chicken strips and asparagus if you prefer.

An easy-to-prepare, elegant salad, enhanced
with a warm Oriental-flavoured dressing.

Citrus roast chicken

Serves 4

1 oven-ready chicken, about
 1.6kg/3½lb
olive oil, for brushing
2 tsp five peppercorn mixture,
 crushed
3 tbsp redcurrant jelly
juice of 1 pink grapefruit
pink grapefruit segments, to
 garnish

1 Preheat oven to 200C/fan oven 180C/Gas 6. Brush the chicken all over with olive oil, then sprinkle with the crushed pepper and salt. Place breast side down in a non-metal shallow ovenproof dish. Roast for 45 minutes.
2 Melt the redcurrant jelly in a pan over a low heat. Add the grapefruit juice and bring to the boil, stirring. Turn chicken breast side up and spoon over half of the glaze. Lower oven setting to 180C/fan oven 160C/Gas 4 and roast chicken for a further 45 minutes, or until cooked through, basting at intervals with more glaze.
3 Transfer the chicken to a serving dish, cover loosely with foil and rest in a warm place for 15 minutes. Skim off the oil from the pan juices and heat until bubbling.
4 Serve the chicken garnished with grapefruit segments, with the pan juices as a gravy.

Notes To calculate roasting time, allow about 20 minutes per 500g/1lb weight plus an extra 20 minutes at 200C/fan oven 180C/Gas 6.
To test that the chicken is thoroughly cooked, pierce the thickest part of the leg with a skewer and make sure that the juices run clear, not at all pink.

An original roast – flavoured with crushed mixed peppercorns and a fresh grapefruit and redcurrant glaze.

Sesame roast chicken

Serves 4

1 oven-ready chicken, about
   1.6kg/3½lb
3 tbsp sesame oil
3 tbsp soy sauce
2–3 tsp grated fresh root ginger
1 tsp sesame seeds

1 Preheat oven to 200C/fan oven 180C/Gas 6. Mix the sesame oil, soy sauce and ginger together and brush half inside and over the chicken.
2 Lay the chicken breast down in the roasting tin and roast for 45 minutes. Turn breast up and brush with more soy mixture. Roast for 20 minutes.
3 Brush over the last of the soy mixture, sprinkle with sesame seeds and roast for a further 25 minutes or until the chicken is cooked, reducing the setting to 180C/fan oven 160C/Gas 4 if the bird is browning too fast.

Note Roasting the chicken breast-side down to start with helps to keep the breast meat succulent and moist.

This oriental style roast is delicious served with ready-made plum sauce and a salad of shredded cucumber and spring onion.

Mango and chicken salad

Serves 4
4 cooked chicken breasts (preferably roasted)
2 large mangoes, peeled, halved and stoned
50g/2oz roasted cashew nuts
½ head of iceberg lettuce, shredded

For the dressing
120ml/4fl oz coconut milk
½ tsp ground coriander
1 tbsp Thai fish sauce
1 tbsp soft brown sugar
2 spring onions, finely sliced
1 tbsp finely chopped fresh mint
2 tsp finely chopped fresh lemon grass
salt and pepper

1 First make the dressing. Put the ingredients in a small pan and heat gently until the sugar is dissolved. Remove from the heat and set aside.
2 Cut the chicken and mango flesh into cubes or slices and place in a large bowl with the cashew nuts. Toss to mix.
3 Divide the shredded lettuce between plates and top with the chicken and mango mixture. Stir the dressing and pour over the salad to serve.

Variation Use paw paw (papayas) instead of mangoes.

Scented mango, roast chicken, cashew nuts and crisp lettuce in a Thai coconut dressing, flavoured with fresh mint and lemon grass.

Smoky chicken wings

Serves 4

12 large chicken wings
2 tbsp olive oil
juice of ½ lemon
2 tsp sweet chilli sauce
1 tsp Pimenton (smoked Spanish
    paprika) or sweet paprika
1 tbsp sun-dried tomato paste or
    tomato purée
1 garlic clove, crushed
salt and pepper
thyme sprigs, to garnish

1 Pre-soak 8 long wooden or bamboo skewers in cold water for 20 minutes.
Mix the olive oil, lemon juice, chilli sauce, paprika, tomato paste and garlic
together to form a thick sauce.
2 Preheat the grill (or barbecue). Cut off the very tips of the chicken wings.
Thread 3 chicken wings onto 2 parallel skewers; repeat with the remaining
wings and skewers.
3 Grill (or barbecue) for 15 minutes, turning twice, then brush liberally
with the sauce. Grill (or barbecue) for a further 10–15 minutes until cooked
through and nicely browned, turning and basting with the sauce from time
to time.
4 Season and garnish with thyme to serve. Eat the chicken wings with your
fingers!

Note The secret of these barbecued wings is to brush with the glaze towards
the end of cooking rather than at the start, to avoid scorching them.

Grill or barbecue these spicy sweet-sour glazed
chicken wings and serve with warm bread and
a tomato salad.

Mexican enchiladas

Serves 4

2 tbsp olive oil

2 red peppers, seeded and thinly
 sliced

2 red onions, sliced

3 cloves garlic, crushed

2 red chillies, seeded and finely
 sliced

2 tsp ground coriander

2 tsp ground cumin

4 chicken breast fillets, cut into
 strips

salt and pepper

220g can refried beans

4 tbsp chopped fresh coriander

300ml/½ pint soured cream

8 flour tortillas

140g/5oz mature Cheddar cheese,
 grated

1 Heat the oil in a large pan, then add the peppers, onions, garlic and
three quarters of the chilli. Stir-fry over a high heat for about 8 minutes
until softened.

2 Stir in the ground spices, then add the chicken strips and seasoning.
Cover and cook for 5 minutes.

3 Remove from the heat and stir in the refried beans, three quarters
of the fresh coriander and 2 tbsp of the soured cream.

4 Lay the tortillas on a work surface. Divide the chicken mixture between
them and roll up to enclose. Place in a large ovenproof dish and top with
the remaining soured cream. Scatter over the cheese, remaining chilli and
coriander. (If preparing ahead, cover and chill.)

5 When ready to serve, preheat oven to 190C/fan oven 170C/Gas 5. Cover the
tortilla dish with foil and bake for 50 minutes. Remove the foil and bake for
a further 10–15 minutes until golden and piping hot. Serve with an avocado
and lettuce salad.

Spicy Mexican tortillas are filled with chicken,
refried beans and coriander, then baked in
soured cream with a cheese and chilli topping.

Chicken on a bed of bay leaves

Serves 4
2 tbsp olive oil
20 fresh bay leaves
4 skinless chicken breast fillets
salt and pepper

1 Heat the oil gently in a heavy-based pan or casserole. Cover the base
of the pan with a layer of bay leaves, then lay the chicken breast fillets
on top. Season, cover tightly and cook for 10–12 minutes.
2 Turn the chicken breasts over, re-cover and cook for a further 10 minutes
or until cooked through. Serve the chicken with the pan juices and
vegetables of your choice.

This unusual Italian way of cooking chicken
imparts a unique flavour.

Chorizo and chicken gumbo

Serves 4
3 tbsp olive oil
2 tbsp plain flour
2 fresh bay leaves
1 large onion, finely chopped
4 celery sticks, thickly sliced
1 tbsp Cajun seasoning
1 tsp fresh thyme leaves
400g can peeled tomatoes in juice

700ml/1¼ pints chicken stock
2 large green peppers, seeded and
 cubed
140g/5oz okra, trimmed (halved if
 large)
8 skinless chicken thighs
200g/7oz piece chorizo sausage,
 skinned and diced
salt and pepper

1 Heat the oil in a large heavy-based pan or flameproof casserole. Stir in the flour and bay leaves and cook gently for about 5 minutes, stirring frequently until the flour is a nutty brown colour.
2 Tip in the onion and celery and cook gently for 5 minutes. Stir in the Cajun seasoning and thyme leaves.
3 Pour in the tomatoes and stock, then stir in all the remaining ingredients, seasoning with salt and pepper to taste. Cover and simmer for 40 minutes until the chicken is tender. (If preparing ahead, cool and chill.)
4 When ready to serve, reheat on the hob until piping hot. Serve with mixed basmati and wild rice or bread and a leafy salad.

Spicy Spanish chorizo gives this New Orleans stew a rich flavour. Okra is an authentic ingredient of gumbo and its sticky juices help to thicken the sauce.

Prawn and chicken laksa

Serves 4

1 tbsp vegetable oil
1 onion, finely chopped
2 tsp grated fresh root ginger
2 tsp crushed garlic
3 lemon grass stalks, finely chopped
1 tbsp ground coriander
2 tsp ground cumin
1 red chilli, seeded and thinly sliced
4 boneless chicken thighs, skinned
  and cut into bite size pieces

400ml/14fl oz coconut milk
200ml/7fl oz chicken stock
200g/7oz cooked peeled tiger prawns
6 tbsp finely chopped fresh
  coriander
salt and pepper
200g/7oz packet medium egg
  noodles

1 Heat the oil in a large heavy-based pan, add the onion, ginger, garlic and lemon grass, and cook gently until the onion is softened.
2 Add the ground coriander and cumin and stir-fry for 1 minute, then add the chilli and chicken. Stir-fry for 2–3 minutes, then pour in the coconut milk and stock. Bring to a simmer and cook gently for 15–20 minutes. Stir in the prawns and coriander leaves; season.
3 Meanwhile cook the noodles according to the pack instructions; drain well. Divide between serving bowls and top with the prawn mixture to serve.

Fragrant lemon grass, spicy red chilli, fresh ginger and pungent coriander gives this Thai dish its distinctive character.

simple
meat

Lamb chops with sweet potatoes and garlic

Serves 4

4 lean chump chops or 8 lamb
  cutlets
4 tbsp olive oil
1kg/2¼lb sweet potatoes, peeled and
  cubed
2 red onions, cut into wedges
8 garlic cloves (unpeeled)

1 tbsp light muscovado sugar
juice of 1 lemon
1 small lemon, halved and thinly
  sliced
1 tbsp fresh thyme leaves, plus
  8 sprigs
salt and pepper

1 Trim the lamb of any excess fat. Preheat oven to 220C/fan oven 200C/Gas 7.
2 Heat the olive oil in a large frying pan. Add the sweet potato cubes, onion
wedges, garlic and sugar and fry, stirring, over a high heat for about
5 minutes until the vegetables start to soften and caramelise. Transfer
to a roasting tin.
3 Add the lemon juice, lemon slices, thyme leaves and seasoning, then top
with the lamb chops and thyme sprigs.
4 Roast in the oven for 25–30 minutes until the lamb chops are cooked and
the sweet potatoes are tender. Serve garnished with thyme sprigs and
accompanied by spinach.

Sweet potatoes are sautéed with lemon, red
onions and fresh thyme, then topped with
lamb chops and quick roasted.

Lamb tagine

Serves 4

2 tbsp vegetable oil
1 large onion, finely chopped
2 garlic cloves, finely chopped
1kg/2¼lb boned shoulder of lamb,
   cut into 5cm/2in cubes
1 tsp saffron threads

1 tsp ground ginger
850ml/1½ pints lamb stock or water
250g/9oz ready-to-eat dried prunes
250g/9oz ready-to-eat dried apricots
2 tsp ground cinnamon
2 tbsp clear honey
salt and pepper

1 Heat the oil in a heavy based pan or flameproof casserole and sauté the onion and garlic until soft. Add the meat and fry, turning occasionally, until evenly browned.
2 Add the saffron, ginger and stock or water and stir well. Cover and simmer gently for 1½ hours or until the meat is tender, adding a little hot water if the stew appears to be a little too dry.
3 Add the prunes, apricots, cinnamon and honey. Season with salt and pepper to taste, re-cover and simmer for a further 15 minutes.
4 Taste and adjust the seasoning. Serve with steamed couscous or rice, and a salad or green vegetable.

A wonderful Moroccan stew of lamb and dried fruit, enriched with saffron, ginger, cinnamon and honey.

Creole meatballs

Serves 4
600g/1lb 5oz lean minced lamb
1 onion, finely chopped
3 tbsp plain flour
1 tsp hot paprika
salt and pepper
oil for shallow-frying

For the creole sauce
1 tbsp vegetable oil
1 onion, finely chopped
2 red peppers, cored, seeded and
  chopped
3 garlic cloves, finely chopped
400g can chopped tomatoes
1 bay leaf
200g/8oz fresh pineapple, roughly
  cubed
200ml/7fl oz water

1 For the meatballs, put the minced lamb, onion, flour, paprika and seasoning in a bowl and mix thoroughly. With wet hands, divide the mixture equally into 16 pieces and shape into balls.
2 Heat the oil in a large frying pan and carefully fry the meatballs, turning until evenly browned. Drain on crumpled kitchen paper and set aside. Preheat oven to 200C/fan oven 180C/Gas 6.
3 To make the creole sauce, heat the oil in a frying pan and gently fry the onion until softened. Add the red peppers and garlic; stir-fry for 1 minute. Add the remaining ingredients, season well and bring to the boil, stirring.
4 Put the meatballs in a shallow ovenproof dish. Pour over the sauce and bake in the oven for 20–25 minutes. Serve with plain boiled rice and a crisp green salad.

Tender lamb meatballs cooked in a mildly spiced creole sauce with fresh pineapple and red peppers.

Bobotie

Serves 6–8
1 tbsp vegetable oil
1 large onion, finely chopped
2 garlic cloves, finely chopped
1 kg/2¼lb lean minced lamb
2 tsp ground coriander
1 tsp ground cumin
1 tsp paprika
85g/3oz fresh white breadcrumbs
2 tbsp white wine vinegar

2 eggs, beaten
4 tbsp sultanas
4 tbsp apricot jam
salt and pepper
For the topping
2 eggs
200ml/7fl oz double cream
2 tbsp chopped fresh coriander
  leaves
coriander sprigs, to garnish

1 Line a 23cm/9in loose bottomed cake tin with non-stick baking parchment.
Preheat oven to 180C/fan oven 160C/Gas 4.
2 Heat the oil in a large non-stick frying pan, add the onion and garlic and
fry gently until lightly browned. Add the meat and fry, stirring occasionally,
until browned.
3 Take off the heat and mix in the spices, breadcrumbs, vinegar, beaten eggs,
sultanas, apricot jam and salt to taste. Turn the mixture into the prepared
tin and spread evenly.
4 For the topping, beat the eggs and cream together in a bowl; season well,
then pour the mixture over the meat. Scatter the chopped coriander over the
surface. Stand the cake tin on a baking sheet and bake for 1 hour.
5 Carefully unmould the bobotie. Serve cut into wedges and garnished with
coriander sprigs.

Serve this spicy Cape Malay meatloaf with
yoghurt, naan bread and a salad.

Rump steaks with wilted rocket

Serves 4
4 rump steaks, each 175g/6oz
For the marinade
5 tbsp red wine
2 garlic cloves, crushed
3 tbsp olive oil
salt and pepper

For the aioli
2 garlic cloves, peeled and crushed
1 egg yolk
3 tbsp walnut oil
100ml/3½fl oz light olive oil
lemon juice, to taste
To serve
100g/4oz rocket leaves

1 In a shallow dish, mix together the wine, garlic, olive oil and seasoning. Add the rump steaks and turn to coat well. Cover and leave to marinate for 30 minutes.

2 Meanwhile, make the aioli. Pound the garlic with 1 tsp salt in a small bowl. Stir in the egg yolk. Gradually whisk in the oils, a few drops at a time. Once half the oil is incorporated, add a squeeze of lemon juice. Whisk in remaining oil in a thin, steady stream. Taste and season or add lemon juice as required.

3 Remove steaks from marinade and pat dry on kitchen paper. Brush with a little olive oil. Preheat grill to medium. Put the steaks on the grill rack and cook for 3 minutes each side, or to taste.

4 Serve each steak topped with a pile of rocket leaves and accompanied by the aioli.

Note To barbecue, cook over medium hot coals for 2–3 minutes per side, or to taste.

Tender, marinated rump steaks served topped with rocket and accompanied by a delicious aioli – made with walnut oil.

Horseradish-crusted roast beef

Serves 4–6
1.3kg/3lb boned, rolled rib of beef
salt and pepper
3 tbsp fresh breadcrumbs
2 tbsp hot horseradish sauce
2 tsp grated horseradish

1 Preheat oven to 200C/fan oven 180C/Gas 6. Pat the joint dry with kitchen paper if necessary. Season with salt and pepper.
2 Mix the remaining ingredients together to make a paste, then spread evenly all over the joint.
3 Put the meat into a roasting tin and roast in the oven for 45 minutes. Reduce oven setting to 180C/fan oven 160C/Gas 4 and roast for a further 45 minutes. Rest in a warm place for 10 minutes before carving. Serve with roast potatoes and vegetables of your choice.

Note Always bring a roasting joint to room temperature before cooking, as this will affect the timing.

The best partner for a beautifully cooked roast is a very sharp carving knife – it will make the meat go much further!

Beef with bacon, thyme and garlic

Serves 4–6

1.3kg/3lb boned, rolled sirloin or rib of beef

85g/3oz smoked bacon lardons

3 garlic cloves, cut lengthwise into wedges

15 small fresh thyme sprigs

salt and pepper

olive oil, for basting

1 Preheat oven to 200C/fan oven 180C/Gas 6. Cut about 15 slits in the beef with a sharp knife and insert a piece of bacon, a wedge of garlic and a thyme sprig into each one.

2 Season the joint all over with salt and pepper and rub with a little olive oil.

3 Roast in the oven for 1½–2 hours until cooked to your preference. Leave to rest in a warm place for 10 minutes before carving. Serve with roasted new potatoes and a selection of vegetables.

Note For a succulent roast, look for a joint with a good marbling of fat as this will help to keep the meat moist during roasting.

Boned and rolled sirloin or rib of beef studded with lardons, garlic slivers and thyme sprigs.

Corned beef hash cakes

Serves 4

4 tbsp sunflower oil
1 onion, halved and thinly sliced
1 red pepper, quartered, cored,
  seeded and thinly sliced
2 garlic cloves, sliced
550g/1¼ lb potatoes (unpeeled),
  coarsely grated

6 large eggs
2 tsp Worcestershire sauce
dash of Tabasco sauce
salt and pepper
4 spring onions, finely chopped
200g can corned beef, diced

1 Heat half of the oil in a large frying pan. Add the onion, red pepper, garlic and potatoes and fry, stirring, for 8 minutes until softened.

2 In a large bowl, beat 2 eggs with the Worcestershire sauce, Tabasco and seasoning. Add the potato mixture, spring onions and corned beef; mix together thoroughly. Divide into 4 portions and shape roughly into round cakes.

3 Heat the remaining oil in the frying pan. Add the potato cakes, cover and cook for 10 minutes. Turn the potato cakes over and cook for a further 5 minutes.

4 Meanwhile, poach the remaining 4 eggs in boiling salted water for 3 minutes or until cooked to your liking; lift out with a slotted spoon.

5 Serve the hash cakes topped with the poached eggs, and an extra few drops of Tabasco if liked.

Note If you do not have a frying pan large enough to hold all four hash cakes, use two pans rather than cook in batches.

This unusual, tasty supper also makes a great Sunday brunch. Serve a refreshing leafy salad to follow.

Bean casserole with chorizo

Serves 4

250g/9oz dried pinto beans
100g/4oz dried butter beans
1 tbsp olive oil
450g/1lb pickling or baby onions,
  peeled
225g/8oz thick smoked gammon
  steak, cubed
200g/7oz chorizo sausage, skinned
  and cut into chunks

1 each green and orange pepper,
  cored, seeded and cut into chunks
700g bottle or carton passata
425ml/¾ pint chicken stock
3 tbsp molasses
2 tbsp wholegrain mustard
4 fresh bay leaves
1 tbsp fresh thyme leaves
1 tsp paprika

1 Soak the pinto and butter beans separately in plenty of cold water overnight.
2 The next day, rinse the beans ad place in separate large pans. Add fresh
cold water to cover and bring to the boil. Fast boil the butter beans for
10 minutes; pinto beans for 20 minutes. Drain.
3 Heat the oil in a large pan. Add the whole onions and fry over a medium
heat for about 5 minutes, stirring frequently.
4 Add the gammon, chorizo and peppers and cook, stirring, for 3–4 minutes.
Pour in the passata and stock, then stir in the beans, molasses, mustard,
herbs and paprika. Cover and simmer gently, stirring often, for 45 minutes
or until the beans are tender. (If preparing ahead, cool, then chill.)
5 To serve, reheat in a pan over medium heat, if necessary, until piping hot.
Serve with garlic bread and a salad.

Molasses and spicy chorizo sausage gives this
rustic dish a wonderful depth of flavour.

Mexican beef stew with lime and chilli

Serves 4

3 tbsp vegetable oil
700g/1½lb lean minced beef
1 large onion, finely chopped
1 green chilli, thinly sliced
4 tbsp lime juice
400g can chopped tomatoes
2 Granny Smith's apples, peeled,
  cored and roughly chopped

2 tbsp capers
salt and pepper
3 large potatoes, peeled and cut into
  2cm/¾in cubes
1 garlic clove, finely chopped
2 tsp ground cumin
grated Cheddar cheese, to garnish

1 Heat 2 tbsp oil in a large heavy based frying pan. Add the beef and onion and fry, stirring, until the meat is browned.

2 Add the chilli, lime juice, tomatoes, apples and capers. Lower the heat, cover with a tight fitting lid and simmer for 25 minutes or until the meat is tender. Season to taste.

3 Par-boil the potatoes in salted water for 10 minutes; drain thoroughly.

4 Heat the remaining oil in a large, non-stick frying pan. Add the potatoes, garlic and cumin and fry, stirring, until golden brown.

5 Divide the spiced potatoes between warmed plates and top with the stew. Sprinkle with some grated cheese and serve with tortillas or crusty bread and a salad.

Known as picadillo in Mexico, this unusual stew is flavoured with fresh chilli, lime juice, apples and cumin. It is served on a bed of fried potatoes and topped with cheese.

Spiced pork escalopes with apricots

Illustrated on previous pages

Serves 2–3
450g/1lb pork fillet (tenderloin), cut
   into 1cm/½in slices
1 tsp powdered cloves
salt and pepper
6 fresh apricots, stoned and
   quartered
3 whole cloves
6 tbsp water
2 tsp clear honey

1 Lay the pork slices between sheets of greaseproof paper and beat with a rolling pin to flatten. Sprinkle with the ground cloves, salt and pepper.
2 Heat a large non-stick frying pan until very hot. Cook the pork in batches for about 1 minute each side until tender; transfer to a warmed dish, cover and keep warm in a low oven while cooking the sauce.
3 Add the apricots and whole cloves to the pan and cook, shaking the pan, for 2–3 minutes until they are lightly singed. Add the water and honey, scraping up the sediment. Continue to cook until the apricots are softened but still hold their shape, adding a little more water if needed.
4 Serve the meat topped with the apricots and pan juices. Accompany with French beans or steamed courgettes.

Variations Use fresh plums or crisp apple wedges instead of apricots.

Tender pork fillet, beaten thin, cooks quickly without losing its juiciness. Fresh apricots spiced with cloves are the perfect foil.

French-style bacon steaks

Serves 4

1½ tbsp sunflower oil
4 thick mild cure bacon steak
   rashers
2 small red apples, cored and cut
   into wedges
2 tbsp Calvados or brandy
1 tsp green peppercorns in brine,
   crushed
2 tsp Dijon mustard
200ml carton crème fraîche

1 Heat the oil in a large frying pan and fry the bacon steaks for about
3 minutes, turning once. Lift from the pan; set aside.
2 Add the apples to the pan and sauté for 1 minute or until beginning to
colour. Add the Calvados, then stir in the peppercorns, mustard and crème
fraîche to make a creamy sauce.
3 Return the bacon steaks to the pan to heat through before serving. Serve
with mashed potatoes and stir-fried cabbage.

A chunky apple sauce spiked with Calvados,
Dijon mustard and green peppercorns cuts the
richness of smoked bacon steaks.

Spiced crisp belly pork

Serves 4–6
1.25kg–1.3kg/2¾–3lb piece belly
  pork, boned
salt
1 tsp Thai seven spice mix
300g/10oz shallots, finely sliced
6 garlic cloves, finely chopped

2 fat red chillies, seeded and finely
  chopped
2 tbsp sunflower oil
4 tbsp clear honey
100ml/3½fl oz white wine
3 tbsp dark soy sauce
coriander sprigs, to garnish

1 Using a very sharp knife, deeply score the pork skin through to the fat
at 1cm/½in intervals. Rub in plenty of salt and leave to draw out moisture
for 1–1½ hours.
2 Preheat oven to 200C/fan oven 180C/Gas 6. Dry the pork skin well with
kitchen paper and rub in the spice mix. Place in a shallow roasting tin and
roast for 25 minutes. Mix the shallots, garlic and chillies with the oil.
3 Spoon the shallot mixture under the pork and roast for 50 minutes
or until the skin is very crisp.
4 Brush with 2 tbsp honey and return to the oven for 10 minutes. Brush
with another 1 tbsp honey; roast for a final 10 minutes.
5 Transfer the pork and shallots to a serving plate and rest in a warm place
until the sauce is ready. Pour off the fat from the tin, place on the hob and
add the wine, soy and remaining honey, stirring to deglaze.
6 Cut the meat into squares. Serve on a bed of rice, with the sauce and
shallots. Garnish with coriander sprigs.

This is perfect with steamed bok choi and
sticky Thai rice. Buy organic belly pork if you
can – its thick skin is easier to score.

Hickory and maple ribs

Serves 4
8 meaty pork ribs, about 1.3kg/
  3lb in total
For the marinade
125ml/4fl oz maple syrup
3 tbsp hickory barbecue sauce
juice of 1 small lemon
1 tbsp sweet chilli sauce
2 garlic cloves, crushed

1 Put the pork ribs in a shallow non-metallic dish. Mix all the marinade ingredients together in a bowl, then pour the mixture over the ribs and turn to coat well. Cover and leave to marinate in the fridge for up to 2 days.
2 Preheat oven to 190C/fan oven 170C/Gas 5. Transfer the ribs to a large, shallow roasting tin and baste with the marinade. Cover the tin loosely with foil and bake for 40 minutes, then uncover and bake for a further 40 minutes, basting occasionally, until the meat is tender.
3 Serve the pork ribs accompanied by jacket potatoes and coleslaw or warm bread and a leafy green salad.

Variation Replace the marinade with a hot, spicy sauce. Mix together 6 tbsp tomato ketchup, 4 tbsp Worcestershire sauce, 2 tbsp Dijon mustard, 4 tbsp muscovado sugar and a dash of Tabasco sauce. Marinate the ribs in the mixture and cook as above. Serve with garlic bread and a salad.

Smoky hickory sauce and maple syrup enhance meaty spare ribs to delicious effect.

simple
vegetables
and
salads

Sabzi pulao

Serves 4
400g/14oz basmati rice
2 tbsp vegetable oil
1 onion, halved and thinly sliced
6 cardamom pods
6 cloves
1 cinnamon stick
225g/8oz mushrooms, roughly
  chopped

2 carrots, cut into cubes
1 red pepper, cored, seeded and
  roughly chopped
225g/8oz frozen peas
1 tsp saffron threads, soaked in
  2 tsp hot water
salt and pepper
crisp fried onion slices, to garnish

1 Rinse the rice in a large sieve under cold running water until the water
is clear; drain thoroughly.
2 Heat the oil in a large heavy based pan and sauté the onion over a medium
heat until lightly browned.
3 Add the cardamom pods, cloves and cinnamon. Stir-fry for 1 minute, then
add the rice and fry, stirring, for a further 1 minute. Add the vegetables and
stir well.
4 Stir in 750ml/1¼ pints boiling water, the infused saffron and seasoning.
Cover tightly. Simmer on a very low heat for 15 minutes.
5 Leave to stand, covered, for 10 minutes then fluff up the rice with a fork.
Serve garnished with crisp fried onions.

Serve this one-pot meal with hot pickles,
yoghurt and a cucumber and tomato salsa.

Radicchio, asparagus and black beans

Serves 4

500g/1lb 2oz thin asparagus, trimmed to 13cm/5in lengths
2 radicchio, each cut into 6 wedges
4 garlic cloves, crushed
½ tsp dried chilli flakes

8 tbsp extra virgin olive oil
salt and pepper
200g/7oz cooked black beans (see note), or canned black, aduki or red kidney beans
4 tsp balsamic vinegar

1 Put the asparagus and radicchio in a large shallow dish. Add the garlic, chilli flakes, 4 tbsp oil and seasoning. Turn the vegetables to coat well.
2 Preheat a ridged griddle pan or heavy based frying pan over a medium heat, then cook the asparagus for 2 minutes on each side. Return to the dish.
3 Add the radicchio to the pan and cook for 1 minute each side; add to the asparagus.
4 Put the black beans in a pan with some of their liquid. Warm through, then drain and add to the vegetables. Toss to mix and check the seasoning.
5 Serve warm or cold, drizzled with the balsamic vinegar and remaining oil.

Note To obtain this weight of cooked beans, soak 100g/4oz dried black beans in cold water overnight. Drain, put into a pan and cover with fresh water. Bring to the boil and boil fast for 10 minutes, then lower the heat and simmer for 1¼ hours or until tender.

This wonderful combination of flavours is perfect for a vegetarian meal. Serve warm or cold, with char-grilled flat bread if you like.

Bubble and squeak cake

Illustrated on previous pages

Serves 3–4

1kg/2¼lb potatoes, peeled and cubed
450g/1lb green cabbage, cored and
  shredded
2 leeks, thinly sliced
1 tsp salt
1 tsp coarsely ground black pepper

50g/2oz butter
200ml/7fl oz milk
140g/5oz chorizo sausage, skinned
  and chopped (optional)
2 tbsp sunflower oil
chopped parsley, to garnish

1 Add the potatoes to a large pan of boiling salted water, bring to the boil and position a steamer on top. Put the cabbage and leeks in the steamer and cook for 20 minutes.

2 Drain the potatoes and mash with the seasoning, butter and milk until smooth and creamy. Stir in the cabbage, leeks and chorizo sausage if using. Allow to cool. (If preparing ahead, cover and chill.)

3 To cook, heat 1 tbsp oil in a large heavy based frying pan. Add the potato mixture and press down evenly to make a cake. Fry over a medium heat for 10 minutes.

4 Turn the cake out on to a large plate. Heat the remaining oil in the frying pan, then slide the potato cake back into the pan and fry the other side for 5–10 minutes until golden and heated through. Serve at once, scattered with plenty of chopped parsley and accompanied by grilled tomatoes.

Spanish chorizo adds a unique flavour to this traditional dish, but it can be omitted for vegetarians.

Cracked wheat pilaf, chestnuts and fennel

Serves 4
4 red onions, peeled with root end
  intact
4 small fennel bulbs, trimmed with
  root end intact
6 tbsp olive oil
salt and pepper

250g/9oz cracked (bulgar) wheat
700ml/1¼ pints well flavoured
  vegetable stock (preferably
  homemade)
200g/7oz cooked peeled chestnuts
3 tbsp chopped flat leaf parsley

1 Preheat oven to 220C/fan oven 200C/Gas 7. Cut each onion and fennel bulb lengthways into 6–8 pieces. Place on a baking tray and drizzle with half of the oil. Season with salt and pepper and turn well to coat the vegetables with the oil.
2 Rinse the cracked wheat and drain well. Heat 2 tbsp oil in a heavy based flameproof casserole. Add the cracked wheat and stir to coat with the oil. Pour in the stock and bring to the boil. Lower the heat, cover and simmer gently for 15–20 minutes.
3 Meanwhile, roast the vegetables in the oven for 20 minutes.
4 When the cracked wheat is ready, turn off the heat, remove the lid and cover with a clean tea towel or muslin.
5 Add the chestnuts to the vegetables, turn to coat with oil and return to the oven for a further 5 minutes. Fold the vegetables into the cracked wheat with the remaining 1 tbsp oil and the chopped parsley to serve.

Variation Serve the pilaf cold, with a herb vinaigrette folded through.

A simple, flexible vegetarian meal. Try using a mixture of herbs, add canned aduki beans or scatter with toasted pine nuts.

Warm mushroom, ham and sweet potato salad

Serves 2

25g/1oz butter

1 small sweet potato, peeled and diced

100g/4oz small chestnut mushrooms, halved

80g pkt Black Forest ham, each slice halved

50g/2oz baby spinach leaves

25g/1oz watercress sprigs

For the dressing

3 tbsp extra virgin olive oil

1 tbsp tarragon or red wine vinegar

1 garlic clove, crushed

1 tsp chopped fresh tarragon

1 tbsp chopped fresh basil

salt and pepper

To garnish

basil sprigs

1 Melt the butter in a frying pan, add the sweet potato and fry, stirring frequently, for 8–10 minutes until tender and golden.

2 Meanwhile, mix the dressing ingredients together in a bowl, seasoning with salt and pepper to taste.

3 Remove sweet potato from the pan; keep warm. Add the mushrooms to the pan and fry for 3–4 minutes until softened. Add the ham and cook for 1–2 minutes.

4 Put the spinach and watercress on to serving plates. Scatter with the mushrooms, ham and sweet potato croûtons. Drizzle with the dressing and serve garnished with basil.

Note If Black Forest ham is unobtainable, use Parma ham instead.

A substantial warm salad, topped with sweet potato croûtons.

Chicory, radish and red onion salad

Illustrated on previous pages

Serves 4
4 heads of chicory, cut into chunks
1 bunch red salad radishes,
   quartered
1 red onion, very finely sliced
For the dressing
1 bunch watercress, stalks removed
4 tbsp extra virgin olive oil
1 tbsp white wine vinegar
1 tsp black peppercorns
salt

1 Put the salad ingredients in a bowl of iced water while making the dressing.
2 Whizz the watercress leaves, oil, vinegar and black peppercorns in a blender or food processor until almost smooth. Taste and season with salt – it should be quite peppery.
3 Drain and dry vegetables. Toss with half of the dressing and then place in a salad bowl. Drizzle with remaining dressing to serve.

A crunchy side salad with a vivid green, peppery dressing of puréed watercress.

New potato salad with chervil and chives

Serves 4

675g/1½lb Jersey Royals or other
   new potatoes, scrubbed
salt and pepper
4 tbsp mayonnaise
2 tbsp Greek yoghurt
1 tsp wholegrain mustard
2 tbsp chopped fresh chervil or flat
   leaf parsley
2 tbsp chopped fresh chives
squeeze of lemon juice

1 Add the new potatoes to a pan of cold salted water, bring to the boil and simmer for 12–15 minutes until just tender.
2 Meanwhile, combine the mayonnaise and yoghurt in a large bowl and stir in the mustard. Season with salt and pepper to taste.
3 Drain the potatoes in a colander and cool slightly, then toss with the dressing and chopped herbs while still warm. Add a squeeze of lemon juice and check the seasoning. Serve warm or at room temperature.

Chervil is a delicately flavoured herb that goes well with potatoes; if unobtainable, simply use flat leaf parsley instead.

Baby beets with orange and walnuts

Serves 4

16 baby beetroot with leaves
  (2 bunches)
4 oranges
4 tbsp olive oil
salt and pepper
85g/3oz walnut halves

1 Preheat oven to 190C/fan oven 170C/Gas 5. Cut the tops from the beetroot; set aside. Scrub the beetroot and put in a baking dish.

2 Finely grate the rind from 2 oranges and squeeze the juice. Add this rind and juice to the beetroot with half the olive oil, and seasoning; toss to coat. Cover with foil and bake for 45 minutes or until tender.

3 Meanwhile, peel and segment the remaining oranges, discarding all of the membrane and pips.

4 Heat the remaining oil in a frying pan and add the beetroot tops. Sauté for 2–3 minutes until wilted and tender. Stir in the orange segments and walnuts. Season generously with salt and pepper.

5 Add the baked beetroot to the wilted beet tops. Toss to mix well and then serve immediately.

Young beetroot – bought in bunches – are best baked to retain all their earthy flavour. Combined with orange, walnuts and their leafy tops, they make a great accompaniment.

Spiced roast potatoes with garlic

Serves 4

1.1kg/2½lb potatoes, peeled and cut
  into 5cm/2in chunks
2 tbsp plain flour
1 tbsp smoked paprika or mustard
  powder
1 tsp salt
4 tbsp vegetable oil
2 garlic bulbs, cloves separated
  (unpeeled)

1 Preheat oven to 220C/fan oven 200C/Gas 7. Put the potatoes in a large pan and add cold water to cover. Bring to the boil and boil steadily for 5 minutes. Immediately drain and leave, uncovered, to cool slightly.
2 Mix together the flour, paprika or mustard and salt. Put the oil in a roasting tin and heat in the oven for a minute or two.
3 Meanwhile, toss the potato chunks in the spice mix to coat well. Carefully add to the hot oil, with the garlic cloves. Roast in the oven for 40–50 minutes until the potatoes are crunchy and browned, turning halfway through cooking. Serve piping hot.

Potato cubes, tossed in smoked paprika or mustard powder and roasted in olive oil with whole garlic cloves for a tasty accompaniment.

Roasted tomatoes and pepper salad

Illustrated on previous pages

Serves 4

2 red peppers, halved, cored and
  seeded
2 yellow peppers, halved, cored and
  seeded
6 tbsp olive oil

6 ripe plum tomatoes, quartered and
  cored
12 large garlic cloves (unpeeled)
2 tbsp balsamic vinegar
salt and pepper

1 Preheat oven to 200C/fan oven 180C/Gas 6. Cut each pepper half into 3 or 4 thick strips. Toss with the olive oil and place in a baking tin. Bake for 15 minutes.

2 Stir in the tomatoes and unpeeled garlic cloves and roast for a further 15–20 minutes or until the garlic cloves are soft and the peppers begin to colour.

3 Lift out the roasted vegetables and garlic with a slotted spoon and place in a warm serving dish. Swirl the balsamic vinegar into the pan juices. Bring to the boil and let bubble for 30 seconds, then pour over the tomatoes and peppers.

4 Season with salt and pepper to taste and serve immediately or allow to cool to room temperature; do not refrigerate.

A gutsy, colourful cooked salad inspired by the flavours of the Mediterranean. Serve as an accompaniment to grilled meat or poultry.

Hassleback potatoes

Serves 4

8 even sized, slightly oval potatoes,
  each about 140g/5oz
2 tbsp truffle oil, or extra virgin
  olive oil
1 small bunch (or packet) fresh
  thyme
sea salt

1 Preheat oven to 220C/fan oven 200C/Gas 7. Slice each potato vertically
across its width at 3mm/⅛in intervals, without cutting right through. Rinse,
then put the potatoes in a bowl of chilled water for 15 minutes; they will
open out slightly. Drain and dry well.
2 Brush the oil between the potato slices and all over the skin. Push a small
thyme sprig into each slit. Season with salt.
3 Place each potato on a 20cm/8in square of foil, pull up the corners and
twist loosely. Put the parcels on a baking sheet and bake in the oven for
40 minutes. Fold back the foil slightly and bake for a further 30–40 minutes
until the potatoes are cooked.

These thyme scented, fanned roast potatoes
are excellent with poultry and game.

Bok choi with shiitake mushrooms

Serves 4
600g/1lb 5oz bok choi or pak choi,
    stems removed
2 tbsp vegetable oil
3 large garlic cloves, finely sliced
6 spring onions, finely sliced
350g/12oz shiitake mushrooms,
    thickly sliced

½ tsp coarsely ground black pepper
1½ tbsp caster sugar
1 tsp sesame oil
1 tbsp rice wine or rice wine vinegar
3 tbsp dark soy sauce
To serve
sesame oil, for drizzling (optional)

1 Separate and roughly chop the bok choi leaves. Add to a large pan of
boiling water and cook for 2 minutes; drain thoroughly and set aside.
2 Heat the oil in a large wok. Add the garlic, spring onions, mushrooms and
pepper, and stir-fry for 4–5 minutes.
3 Add the sugar, sesame oil, rice wine and soy sauce. Stir-fry for 2 minutes,
then add the blanched bok choi, toss well and heat through.
4 Serve at once in warmed bowls, drizzled with a little sesame oil if wished
and accompanied by rice or noodles.

Quick and easy Chinese stir-fried vegetables,
flavoured with soy, sesame and rice wine.

Peas with cherry tomatoes and spinach

Illustrated on previous pages

Serves 4

225g/8oz shelled fresh or frozen peas

150ml/¼ pint dry white wine

2 tbsp olive oil

1–2 fresh bay leaves

175g/6oz whole ripe cherry tomatoes

225g/8oz fresh leaf spinach, stalks
  removed (see note)

salt and pepper

1 Place the peas in a large pan with the wine, olive oil and bay leaves. Bring to the boil, then lower the heat and simmer gently for 5 minutes.

2 Add the cherry tomatoes and simmer for a further 5 minutes until tender and the liquid is well reduced.

3 Finally, stir in the spinach and cook for a few minutes, turning occasionally, until the leaves just wilt.

4 Season with salt and pepper to taste. Serve immediately.

Note For convenience, buy bags of ready prepared spinach from supermarkets. Otherwise, choose small, tender spinach leaves and wash thoroughly in several changes of water to remove all traces of grit. Drain thoroughly before cooking.

This is a sort of quick vegetable stew – very colourful and full of goodness! Serve with grilled or roast meat or poultry.

Moroccan spiced cauliflower with mint

Serves 4–6
1 medium cauliflower, divided into
    florets
85g/3oz butter
1 tsp sweet paprika
½ tsp ground cumin
½ tsp ground coriander
salt and pepper
handful of fresh mint leaves

1 Steam the cauliflower over boiling water for 10–12 minutes until just tender. Remove and allow to dry a little.
2 Melt the butter in a frying pan. When sizzling, add the spices and fry, stirring, for 30 seconds. Add the cauliflower florets and stir to coat with the buttery spices. Season well with salt and pepper.
3 Add the mint leaves and cook gently until wilted. Serve immediately.

Cauliflower is lightly steamed until tender, then tossed in a Moroccan spiced melted butter with fresh mint leaves.

simple
desserts
and bakes

White chocolate and berry creams

Serves 4
500g bag frozen mixed summer
   fruits (raspberries, blackberries,
   redcurrants etc.)
3 tbsp icing sugar
4 tsp cassis, framboise or kirsch
200g/7oz white chocolate, in pieces

150g carton whole milk raspberry
   yoghurt
500g carton fromage frais with
   added cream
white chocolate curls or grated
   chocolate, to decorate

1 Tip the frozen fruits into a bowl, stir in the icing sugar, then spoon
into 4 wide stemmed glasses and drizzle over the liqueur.
2 Put the chocolate in a large heatproof bowl over a pan of simmering
water until just melted. Remove from the heat, then beat in the yoghurt
and fromage frais until smooth.
3 Spoon the chocolate mixture over the fruit and leave in a cool place to
allow the fruits to defrost slowly.
4 Serve topped with chocolate curls or grated chocolate.

Tart summer berries under a contrasting
blanket of smooth, creamy white chocolate
are an irresistible combination.

Amaretto and blueberry syllabubs

Serves 4
For the blueberry layer
2 x 170g punnets blueberries
1 tbsp amaretto liqueur
1 tbsp caster sugar
For the syllabub
284ml carton double cream
2 tbsp caster sugar

90ml/3fl oz medium white wine,
  such as Riesling
3 tbsp amaretto liqueur
8 amaretti biscuits, broken into
  small pieces
To decorate
mint leaves

1 Tip the blueberries into a large pan. Add the liqueur and sugar and poach gently for 1–2 minutes until the berries have softened, but have not burst. Allow to cool.

2 To make the syllabub, pour the cream into a bowl. Add the sugar, wine and liqueur, and whisk until the mixture holds its shape.

3 Toss the blueberries with the amaretti biscuits, then layer with the creamy syllabub in 4 stemmed glasses. Chill until required.

4 Serve the chilled syllabubs decorated with mint leaves.

Note Fresh gooseberries, apricots and plums all make excellent alternatives to blueberries. Stone and quarter plums or apricots. Adjust the sugar accordingly and poach until the fruit is tender, but still retaining shape.

Topped with an almond-flavoured syllabub, poached blueberries make an elegant, quick dessert – ideal for mid-week entertaining.

Pan-fried banana with orange and cardamom

Serves 4

50g/2oz unsalted butter
50g/2oz light muscovado sugar
5 cardamom pods, lightly crushed
4 bananas, peeled and halved
   lengthways
grated rind and juice of 1 large
   orange

1 Melt the butter in a large frying pan, then add the sugar with the cardamom and stir until the sugar is dissolved.
2 Add the bananas and cook for 1–2 minutes, turning them in the juices, until softened. Add the orange juice and rind and let bubble until reduced and syrupy. Discard the cardamom pods.
3 Serve hot, with vanilla ice cream.

Cardamom adds an exotic flavour to this hot dessert. Vanilla ice cream is the perfect accompaniment.

Caramelised apples on brioche toasts

Serves 4

3 tbsp caster sugar

3 Cox's apples, peeled, cored and thickly sliced

25g/1oz butter

large pinch of ground cinnamon

3 tbsp raisins

juice of 1 lemon

4 thick slices of brioche (from a large cottage brioche)

250g carton Greek yoghurt

1 Sprinkle the sugar over the base of a large frying pan and heat gently until it melts and begins to caramelise – don't allow to darken.

2 Add the apples and toss to coat, then add the butter, cinnamon, raisins, lemon juice and 1 tbsp water. Cook, turning frequently, for 1–2 minutes.

3 Meanwhile, toast the brioche slices under a hot grill until golden on both sides. Place on serving plates.

4 Spoon the yoghurt on to the brioche and top with the caramelised apples and pan juices to serve.

Butter enriched brioche makes a delicious base for pan-fried apple slices.

Glazed mille feuilles

Serves 4

8 small sheets filo pastry (each about
  21x19cm/12½x7½in)
50g/2oz butter, melted
8 tbsp icing sugar, sifted
115g/4oz mascarpone
4 tsp rosewater essence

150ml/¼ pint double cream
400g/14oz mixed soft fruit, such as
  raspberries, strawberries,
  redcurrants, blueberries and
  blackcurrants
mint leaves, to decorate (optional)

1 Preheat oven to 200C/fan oven 180C/Gas 6. Lay a sheet of filo on a clean
surface (keep the rest covered). Brush with melted butter, then layer 3 more
sheets on top, brushing all except the top sheet with butter. Repeat to make
another stack with the remaining filo.
2 Cut each stack into 6 triangles, it won't matter if they are a little uneven.
Place on baking sheets and dust with approximately 2 tbsp of the icing
sugar. Bake for 10–12 minutes until crisp and golden.
3 Pop under a hot grill (not too close to the element) for 15–30 seconds
to glaze. Transfer to a wire rack to cool.
4 For the filling, beat the mascarpone with 4 tbsp icing sugar and the
rosewater until smooth. Lightly whip the cream in another bowl, then gently
fold into the mascarpone.
5 To assemble, layer 3 filo triangles per serving with mascarpone cream and
fruit. Top with a sprig of redcurrants, and mint leaves if using. Just before
serving, dust with the remaining icing sugar.

Note For convenience, prepare ahead to the end of stage 4. Assemble the
mille feuilles 2 hours before serving.

These impressive filo stacks – layered with
mascarpone and berries – are deceptively easy.

Melon, mint and ginger salad

Serves 8

1 medium Galia melon
1 Charantais or Cantaloupe melon
¼ small watermelon
2.5cm/1in piece fresh root ginger,
  peeled and roughly chopped
1 tbsp freshly torn mint leaves
mint sprigs, to decorate

1 Halve the whole melons. Scoop out the seeds from all 3 melons, then cut the flesh into chunks and place in a large bowl, adding any juices.
2 Put the ginger in a clean garlic press, hold over the melon bowl and press firmly, to extract the ginger juice. Add the mint leaves and toss gently. Chill until required.
3 Just before serving, toss the salad lightly and scatter with mint sprigs.

A refreshing, healthy fruit salad with the zing of freshly pressed ginger. Melons at their peak of ripeness are essential.

Peaches in elderflower champagne

Serves 6–8
6–8 peaches, ripe but firm
100ml/3½fl oz elderflower cordial
375ml/13fl oz (½ bottle) dry
 Champagne or good quality
 sparkling white wine

1 Preheat oven to 200C/fan oven 180C/Gas 6. Arrange the peaches closely in a deep ovenproof dish (just large enough to hold them in a single layer).
2 Measure the elderflower cordial into a jug, add the Champagne or sparkling wine, then pour the mixture over the peaches. Cover the dish with a lid, or with greaseproof paper then a layer of foil to seal.
3 Bake for 40–50 minutes or until the peaches are tender right through. If they are not fully submerged in the liquid, turn them over halfway through the cooking time.
4 Leave the peaches to cool in the syrup. If preferred, lift out and peel off the skins, then return the peaches to the elderflower Champagne to serve.

Luxuriously steeped in Champagne sweetened with a little elderflower cordial, these peaches make a mouth-watering summer dessert.

Raspberry yoghurt ice

Serves 4–6

500g/1lb 2oz raspberries
2 tbsp light muscovado sugar
6 tbsp maple syrup
500ml/18fl oz organic yoghurt

1 Put the raspberries and sugar in a blender or food processor and work to a purée, then pass through a sieve into a bowl to remove the seeds.
2 Stir the maple syrup and yoghurt into the raspberry purée.
3 Freeze in an ice cream maker if you have one, according to the manufacturer's instructions. Alternatively, pour the fruit mixture into a freezerproof container and place in the coldest part of the freezer until partially frozen. As the ice crystals begin to form around the edges, remove the container from the freezer and whisk the raspberry mixture to break up the ice crystals. Return to the freezer. Repeat this process once more, then freeze until firm.
4 If necessary, transfer the yoghurt ice to the fridge 30 minutes before serving to soften.

This wonderfully fresh-tasting ice relies on the use of flavourful, ripe raspberries.

Triple-chocolate brownies

Illustrated on previous pages

Makes about 12

115g/4oz butter, plus extra for
greasing
85g/3oz good quality plain dark
chocolate (minimum 70% cocoa
solids), in pieces
4 medium eggs, beaten
2 tsp vanilla extract

400g/14oz caster sugar
115g/4oz plain flour
25g/1oz cocoa powder
115g packet milk chocolate drops
115g packet white chocolate drops
8 butterscotch sweets, roughly
chopped

1 Preheat oven to 190C/fan oven 170C/Gas 5. Butter a 28x18cm/11x7in
shallow baking tin and line the base with non-stick baking parchment.
2 Melt the butter with the chocolate in a heatproof bowl over a pan of
simmering water. Remove from the heat and stir in the beaten eggs, vanilla
extract and sugar. Mix thoroughly.
3 Sift the flour with the cocoa powder over the mixture, then beat in until
evenly incorporated. Stir in the chocolate chips and butterscotch pieces.
4 Spoon the mixture into the tin and spread evenly. Bake in the middle of
the oven for about 35 minutes until set on the surface, but still moist in the
middle. Leave to cool in the tin.
5 Turn out when completely cold and cut into squares or bars to serve.

Note These chocolate brownies have a characteristic fudge-like texture. For
a more 'cakey' texture, bake for an extra 5–10 minutes.

Irresistible rich, fudgey chocolate brownies,
laden with milk and white chocolate chips,
and butterscotch pieces.

Orange almond cake with rosewater cream

8–10 slices

6 large eggs, separated
175g/6oz caster sugar
grated rind of 2 oranges
juice of 1 orange
225g/8oz ground almonds

For the rosewater cream

2 cardamom pods, seeds extracted
2 tbsp rosewater essence
1 tbsp caster sugar
300ml/½ pint double cream

1 Preheat oven to 180C/fan oven 160C/Gas 4. Grease and base line a 23cm/ 9in spring release cake tin.

2 In a bowl, whisk the egg yolks, sugar and orange rind together until pale and thick. Stir in the orange juice, then fold in the ground almonds.

3 In a clean bowl, whisk the egg whites until just peaking, then fold into the cake mixture.

4 Spoon the mixture into the prepared tin and bake for 45–50 minutes until risen and firm to touch, covering loosely with foil after 20 minutes, if the cake appears to be overbrowning.

5 Meanwhile, for the cream, lightly crush the cardamom seeds and put in a small pan with the rosewater and sugar. Warm gently to dissolve the sugar. Allow to cool, then strain.

6 Whip the cream in a bowl, slowly adding the cooled syrup, until it forms soft peaks.

7 Serve the cake cut into wedges, accompanied by the rosewater cream.

A lovely light almond sponge with a hint of orange, accompanied by an exotic rosewater and cardamom cream.

Lemon polenta cake

8–10 slices

115g/4oz polenta (ordinary or quick-
  cook), plus extra for dusting
115g/4oz plain flour
1½ tsp baking powder
2 large eggs, plus 3 egg whites
175g/6oz caster sugar
grated rind of 2 lemons

125ml/4fl oz lemon juice (juice of
  2–3 lemons)
1 vanilla pod, seeds extracted
100ml/3½fl oz vegetable oil
150ml/¼ pint buttermilk
To serve (optional)
crème fraîche
strawberries

1 Preheat oven to 180C/fan oven 160C/Gas 4. Grease and base line a 25cm/
10in spring release cake tin. Dust the tin out with a little polenta.

2 Sift the flour and the baking powder together into a bowl, then stir
in the polenta.

3 In a separate bowl, whisk the whole eggs, egg whites and sugar together
until pale and thick.

4 Add the polenta mixture, lemon rind and juice, vanilla seeds, oil and
buttermilk. Carefully fold into the whisked mixture, using a large
metal spoon.

5 Spoon the mixture into the prepared tin and bake for 30 minutes, or until
a skewer inserted into the centre comes out clean. Transfer to a wire rack
and leave to cool completely.

6 Cut into slices and serve with crème fraîche and strawberries if you like.

Polenta colours this cake a pretty shade of
yellow and adds a subtle crunch. Strawberries
and crème fraîche are the perfect complement.

Cinnamon chocolate-chip cookies

Illustrated on page 184

Makes 24

140g/5oz butter or margarine, softened
200g/7oz soft brown sugar
50g/2oz caster sugar
2 medium eggs, beaten
350g/12oz plain flour

1 tsp bicarbonate of soda
½ tsp salt
1 tsp ground cinnamon
115g/4oz chopped peanuts
2 x 115g packets plain chocolate drops

1 Preheat oven to 190C/fan oven 170C/Gas 5. Cream the butter and sugars together in a bowl until soft and fluffy. Beat in the eggs.

2 Sift the flour, bicarbonate of soda, salt and cinnamon together over the mixture. Beat well, then stir in the peanuts and chocolate.

3 Drop tablespoonfuls of the mixture well apart on to baking sheets lined with non-stick baking parchment and flatten slightly. Bake for 15–17 minutes until golden.

4 Leave on baking sheets for 10 minutes, then transfer cookies to a wire rack to cool.

Variation Shape smaller cookies if you prefer, reducing the cooking time by 2–3 minutes.

Giant American-style cookies – crisp on the outside, yet meltingly soft within.

Lavender and ginger cookies

Illustrated on page 185

Makes about 36

115g/4oz butter, softened
85g/3oz caster sugar
1 medium egg, beaten
1 tsp vanilla extract
1 tbsp fresh or dried lavender
 flowers (see note)
1 tbsp chopped preserved stem
 ginger

225g/8oz plain flour
¼ tsp bicarbonate of soda
½ tsp baking powder
½ tsp salt
½ tsp ground ginger
50ml/2fl oz soured cream or crème
 fraîche

1 Cream the butter and sugar together in a bowl until soft. Beat in the egg, vanilla and lavender, then fold in the chopped ginger.
2 Sift the flour with the bicarbonate of soda, baking powder, salt and ground ginger. Beat into the mixture, alternately with the soured cream; the dough will be quite soft.
3 Tip the dough on to a sheet of greaseproof paper and gently roll into a cylinder, about 5cm/2in thick. Wrap tightly in cling film and refrigerate for at least 6 hours, preferably overnight.
4 To bake, preheat oven to 190C/fan oven 170C/Gas 5. Slice off thin rounds from the dough as required. Place on baking sheets lined with non-stick baking parchment. Bake for 8–10 minutes until pale golden and set.
5 Cool slightly on the baking sheets, then transfer to a wire rack to cool.

Note If using dried lavender, buy a culinary grade – obtainable from herb suppliers, or dry your own flowers if you have lavender in the garden.

Exquisite fragrant cookies that can be freshly baked to order. Make the dough in advance, keep chilled, then slice and bake as required.

Carrot and raisin cookies

Illustrated on page 185

Makes about 36

225g/8oz freshly cooked carrots, drained
115g/4oz butter or margarine, softened
140g/5oz light muscovado sugar
1 large egg, beaten
400g/14oz plain flour

1½ tsp baking powder
½ tsp ground cinnamon
¼ tsp ground nutmeg
¼ tsp ground ginger
¼ tsp salt
85g/3oz seedless raisins
50g/2oz pecan nuts or walnuts, chopped

1 Preheat oven to 190C/fan oven 170C/Gas 5. Line two baking sheets with non-stick baking parchment. Dry the carrots on kitchen paper, then mash thoroughly until smooth.
2 Cream the butter and sugar together in a bowl. Add the mashed carrot and egg.
3 Sift the flour, baking powder, spices and salt over the mixture, then beat together thoroughly. Stir in the raisins and nuts.
4 Drop teaspoonfuls of the mixture on to the baking sheets, spacing well apart, then flatten the mixture with the back of a wet spoon to shape roughly into rounds. Bake for 12–15 minutes until light golden brown.
5 Leave on the baking sheet for 10 minutes, then transfer to a wire rack to cool completely.

These lightly spiced drop cookies are perfect for lunch boxes.

Vanilla thins

Makes 36

300g/10oz plain flour
1 tsp baking powder
½ tsp salt
2 vanilla pods, split
225g/8oz butter, cubed and softened
225g/8oz caster sugar
1 large egg, beaten

1 Sift the flour together with the baking powder and salt on to a sheet of greaseproof paper.

2 Scrape the seeds from the vanilla pods into the food processor. Add the butter and sugar and process until pale and fluffy. Add the egg and mix until incorporated.

3 Add the sifted flour and process briefly to a soft dough; do not overwork.

4 Turn on to a floured surface and knead lightly. Lift on to greaseproof paper and roll the dough into a cylinder, 5cm/2in thick. Wrap tightly in cling film and refrigerate for at least 6 hours, preferably overnight.

5 To bake, preheat oven to 190C/fan oven 170C/Gas 5. Slice off thin rounds from the dough as required. Place on baking sheets lined with non-stick baking parchment and bake for about 10 minutes until golden and set. Cool slightly on the baking sheets, then transfer to a wire rack to cool.

Note This cookie dough will keep tightly wrapped in the fridge for up to 1 week.

Flavoured with real vanilla seeds, these delicate biscuits make an elegant treat to serve with coffee or ice cream.

Index

Acknowledgements

The publishers wish to thank the following:

Contributors Sara Buenfeld, Maxine Clark, Joanna Farrow, Janet Illsley, Louise Pickford, Bridget Sargeson, Linda Tubby, Sunil Vijayakar
Food Stylists Maxine Clark, Joanna Farrow, Marie Ange Lapierre, Louise Pickford, Bridget Sargeson, Linda Tubby
Photographic Stylists Kasha Harmer Hirst, Maya Babic